WARRIORS OF LIGHT

WARRIORS OF LIGHT

Bruised by the Battles
But Winning the War
against Satan

RANDY BOTT

CFI
An imprint of Cedar Fort, Inc.
Springville, Utah

ISBN 13: 978-1-4621-3823-4

Published by CFI, an imprint of Cedar Fort, Inc.
2373 W. 700 S., Springville, UT 84663
Distributed by Cedar Fort, Inc., www.cedarfort.com

LIBRARY OF CONGRESS CONTROL NUMBER: 2020942633

Cover design by Wes Wheeler

Printed in the United States of America

10 9 8 7 6 5 4 3 2 1

Printed on acid-free paper

Dedication

To the thousands of students and adults who have requested help in conquering the temptations and addictions of a well-experienced adversary.

To my wife, Vickie, and her tireless efforts to encourage me to commit to writing what I have learned by researching the scriptures and latter-day prophets for answers to life's perplexing problems.

To the thousands of courageous "wounded but not defeated" warriors who refuse to give up and continue battling enormous but beatable foes.

Contents

Introduction

Why write a book about the devil and his tactics? Because of his relentless efforts to "make us miserable like unto himself" (2 Nephi 2:18, 27) and his stated objective to "destroy the world" (Moses 4:6).

Identifying the adversary, his strengths, his points of vulnerability, the size of his armies, his weapons, his resources, his objectives, his allies, and the timing of his attacks are just a few of the considerations any wise general would take when planning his defense and his plan of attack to destroy the enemy and win the war.

Even in today's world, wars are being waged, prolonged, and intensified because the enemy has successfully infiltrated our ranks, stolen our strategic plans, and weakened our infrastructure. Traitors have betrayed us at the most critical times, allies have turned against us, and sacred trusts have been destroyed.

In the war against Satan and his hosts, the outcome of that life and death war has been prophetically revealed—he will lose and will be cast into outer darkness forever. The increasing number of spiritual and physical casualties seems, in part, to be the result of people not taking seriously the opposition and their tactics. Others have given up the fight thinking there is no way to win the battles against an enemy who has had over 6000 years' experience and has such seemingly unlimited resources. Still others refuse to acknowledge that there is a devil. They claim that the opposition we are facing is just part of our mortal experience.

This book is written to identify the adversary—past, present, and future—and further identify his tactics with suggested measures we can take to counteract his destructive influence. This is not a comprehensive investigation of either the devil or his tactics but provides a starting place to identify and begin winning the war against Satan.

CHAPTER 1

Winning the War against Satan

SATAN: Who is he?
Where did he come from?
What are his tactics?
What is his destiny?

In today's world, whenever Satan or the devil is mentioned, eyebrows are raised and skeptical smiles are common. Does anyone really believe there is a real arch evil? About 2600 years ago, Nephi of Book of Mormon fame, was shown our day. He recorded,

> And behold, **others he flattereth away, and telleth them there is no hell; and he saith unto them: I am no devil, for there is none**—and thus he whispereth in their ears, until he grasps them with his awful chains, from whence there is no deliverance. (2 Nephi 28:22)

For someone who is called "Satan" 150 times and "the devil" 182 times in the scriptures, it seems apparent that the Savior and His prophets and apostles knew that he is real. But how convenient for the devil to have convinced such a large number of Heavenly Father's children that he really doesn't exist. That allows him and his followers to carry on their work of destroying mankind without fear of being detected. The mythological representations of Satan, even in Christian art, seem to fictionalize his existence rather than portraying him as a real person.

Who is this evil character? Where did he come from? What are his objectives and tactics? And what is his eternal destiny? Coupled with the answers to these questions, efforts will be made to draw from the scriptures the Lord's warnings against the devil and divinely revealed strategies to defeat him. Some scriptures will be used multiple times because of their broad application in identifying and overcoming the influences of Satan.

The Premortal Existence

In order to understand who Satan is, we must look at a time before the earth was created. We all lived in the presence of God, not as mythological creatures but as literal spirit offspring of divine Parents. "All human beings—male and female—are created in the image of God. Each is a beloved spirit son or daughter of heavenly parents, and, as such, each has a divine nature and destiny" ("The Family: A Proclamation to the World," *Ensign* or *Liahona*, Nov. 2010, 129).

For lack of understanding, the Christian world reels at the idea of Satan being a spirit son of Heavenly Father, thus being a spirit brother to Jesus Christ and all of mankind. They offer no explanation of why this cannot be, just that it is a preposterous claim. In his earliest efforts to deceive and destroy mankind, Satan proclaimed that he, along with all of Adam and Eve's children, was a "son of God." "And Satan came among them, saying: I am also a son of God" (Moses 5:13).

The Savior proclaimed His position in that premortal world when He said, "And now, verily I say unto you, I was in the beginning with the Father, and am the Firstborn" (D&C 93:21). Some have gone beyond the scriptures and suggested that Satan, originally named "Lucifer," meaning "light bearer" or "torch bearer," was second born. There is no scriptural basis for such a claim. He was, however, called "a son of the morning" (see D&C 76:26).

Originally, like all mankind, Lucifer was an "intelligence," which, according to what God revealed to Abraham, is the eternal uncreated part of man. He explained to Abraham:

> Howbeit that he made the greater star; as, also, if there be two spirits, and one shall be more intelligent than the other, yet these two spirits, notwithstanding one is more intelligent than the other, have no beginning; they existed before, they shall have no end, they shall exist after, for they are gnolaum, or eternal. (Abraham 3:18)

Further expanding that concept, the Lord revealed to Joseph Smith,

> Man was also in the beginning with God. Intelligence, or the light of truth, was not created or made, neither indeed can be.
>
> All truth is independent in that sphere in which God has placed it, to act for itself, as all intelligence also; otherwise there is no existence. (D&C 93:29–30)

Like every other living thing, Lucifer's intelligence has existed forever. How did he get a spirit body? Likely the same way we all did, by our Heavenly Parents exercising their procreative powers.

Was Lucifer destined to become the archenemy from the time of his spirit birth? It doesn't appear so according to what the Lord said to Joseph Smith in D&C 93:38: "Every spirit of man was innocent in the beginning."

Although not fully explained, Lucifer was influential enough in the pre-earth life to be given "authority," generally accepted to mean he held the priesthood. Joseph Smith and Sidney Rigdon, in viewing a six-part vision that is unparalleled in the amount of light and knowledge it conveys (D&C 76), saw and recorded, "And this we saw also, and bear record, that an angel of God who was in authority in the presence of God . . ." (D&C 76:25).

How did he turn from being one in authority to one who arrogantly sought to dethrone God and Christ? He did it the same way he influenced a third part of his spirit brothers and sisters to join in his rebellion—by exercising agency in opposition to God's revealed plan of salvation for the eternal happiness of all His spirit children. The Lord revealed to Joseph Smith,

> And it came to pass that Adam, being tempted of the devil—for, behold, the devil was before Adam, **for he rebelled against me, saying, Give me thine honor, which is my power; and also a third part of the hosts of heaven turned he away from me because of their agency; And they were thrust down, and thus came the devil and his angels.** (D&C 29:36–37)

We will consider these verses in greater detail later.

God revealed to Moses (after Moses had a face-to-face encounter with Satan) greater details about Satan's fall:

> And I, the Lord God, spake unto Moses, saying: That Satan, whom thou hast commanded in the name of mine Only Begotten, is the same which was from the beginning, and he came before me, saying—Behold,

> here am I, send me, I will be thy son, and I will redeem all mankind, that one soul shall not be lost, and surely I will do it; wherefore give me thine honor.
>
> But, behold, my Beloved Son, which was my Beloved and Chosen from the beginning, said unto me—Father, thy will be done, and the glory be thine forever.
>
> Wherefore, **because that Satan rebelled against me, and sought to destroy the agency of man, which I, the Lord God, had given him, and also, that I should give unto him mine own power;** by the power of mine Only Begotten, I caused that he should be cast down. (Moses 4:1–3)

To ensure that we are understanding the Lord's definition of "the beginning," consider D&C 93:7: "In the beginning, before the world was."

The Lord designated the entire pre-earth life as "in the beginning." It is difficult to comprehend how Lucifer could fall so far and influence so many spirit children of God in an instant. However, there may be a clue in Alma's explanation of why some men became priesthood bearers and others did not qualify. Just for your consideration as a possibility—not intended as a declaration of the doctrine of the Church—consider:

> And this is the manner after which they were ordained—being called and prepared from the foundation of the world according to the foreknowledge of God, on account of their exceeding faith and good works; **in the first place being left to choose good or evil**; therefore they having chosen good, and exercising exceedingly great faith, are called with a holy calling, yea, with that holy calling which was prepared with, and according to, a preparatory redemption for such. (Alma 13:3)

While it is definitely true "being left to choose" could mean "being allowed to choose," it could also mean that we may have resided in a space separated from God's immediate presence to exercise our agency. The rationale being that "no unclean thing can dwell in the presence of God" (see 1 Nephi 10:21; Moses 6:57). Thus, Lucifer could have slowly turned to the dark side, influenced "a third part" of Heavenly Father's children to rebel without allowing his uncleanness to pollute the pure presence of God where "naught but peace, justice, and truth is the habitation of thy throne" (Moses 7:31).

Perhaps you can come up with another explanation, but this one thing is scripturally sure: he did not keep his first estate or his pre-earth life.

> And the Lord said: Whom shall I send? And one answered like unto the Son of Man: Here am I, send me. And another answered and said: Here am I, send me. And the Lord said: I will send the first.
>
> And the second was angry, and kept not his first estate; and, at that day, many followed after him. (Abraham 3:27–28)

Joseph Smith taught,

> The devil has no body, and herein is his punishment. He is pleased when he can obtain the tabernacle of man, and when cast out by the Savior he asked to go into the herd of swine, showing that he would prefer a swine's body to having none. (*Teachings of the Prophet Joseph Smith*, selected by Joseph Fielding Smith [Salt Lake City: Deseret Book, 1976], 181; cf. 297–98)

What was it that was so appealing in Satan's proposed plan that influenced a third part of our spirit siblings to follow him? God explained to Moses,

> And I, the Lord God, spake unto Moses, saying: That Satan, whom thou hast commanded in the name of mine Only Begotten, is the same which was from the beginning, and he came before me, saying—Behold, here am I, send me, **I will be thy son, and I will redeem all mankind, that one soul shall not be lost, and surely I will do it; wherefore give me thine honor.** (Moses 4:1)

That sounds pretty good—salvation without a single soul lost. However, the price was the destruction or surrendering of our agency—the very principle by which exaltation is obtained. "Wherefore, because that Satan **rebelled against me, and sought to destroy the agency of man,** which I, the Lord God, had given him, and also, that I should give unto him mine own power" (Moses 4:3), he was rejected and cast out of heaven. Agency is central to the Father's plan of salvation for His children. Destroy it and there is no plan.

But Satan's arrogant proposal went further than just getting the power of God. Joseph Smith and Sidney Rigdon recorded, "And while we were yet in the Spirit, the Lord commanded us that we should write the vision; for we beheld Satan, that old serpent, even the devil, who rebelled against God, and **sought to take the kingdom of our God and his Christ"** (D&C 76:28).

Perhaps that is one aspect of Satan's rebellion that we have not fully understood. Not only did he rebel against God and Christ, but he also sought to dethrone God. It is difficult to understand how one could be so arrogant and deceive so many when the stakes were so high. Failure meant being banished forever from the presence of God, denied physical bodies, and eventually consigned to outer darkness forever.

However, returning to a closer look at D&C 29:36, the reason for part of his success is revealed. "And it came to pass that Adam, being tempted of the devil—for, behold, the devil was before Adam, for he rebelled against me, saying, **Give me thine honor, which is my power**; and also a third part of the hosts of heaven turned he away from me because of their agency."

When the scripture states that "the devil was before Adam," it does not indicate that he was born in the premortal spirit world before Michael, the arch angel. Adam did not become Adam until he was placed in the Garden of Eden. Before that, he went by his angelic name—Michael. What this verse means is that Satan rebelled before Adam was placed in the Garden of Eden.

But his success did not come by force. It came because of his ability to flatter, deceive, and lie. His followers exercised their agency to their eternal hurt. Continuing His explanation to Moses, God said, "And he became Satan, yea, even the devil, **the father of all lies, to deceive and to blind men, and to lead them captive at his will**, even as many as would not hearken unto my voice" (Moses 4:4).

In castigating Jewish leaders who refused to acknowledge His divine mission, the Savior said, "Ye are of *your* father the devil, and the lusts of your father ye will do. **He was a murderer from the beginning, and abode not in the truth, because there is no truth in him. When he speaketh a lie, he speaketh of his own: for he is a liar, and the father of it**" (John 8:44).

The Savior also recounted the fall of Satan: "And he said unto them, **I beheld Satan as lightning fall from heaven**" (Luke 10:18). John, the Revelator recorded more of the details of Satan's expulsion from heaven:

> And there was **war in heaven**: Michael and his angels fought against the dragon; and the dragon fought and his angels,
>
> And prevailed not; neither was their place found any more in heaven.
>
> And the great dragon was cast out, that old serpent, **called the Devil, and Satan**, which deceiveth the whole world: **he was cast out into the earth, and his angels were cast out with him.** (Revelation 12:7–9)

Only God knows the full reasoning behind Satan and his followers being cast down to the earth. Some have lamented that it would have been for our benefit if they had been cast onto another planet far from us. "But behold, all things have been done in the wisdom of him who knoweth all things" (2 Nephi 2:24).

The Lord, although certainly not beholding to Satan and his followers to accomplish His plans, does use them as part of the testing associated with mortality. The Lord revealed, "And it must needs be that the devil should tempt the children of men, or they could not be agents unto themselves; for if they never should have bitter they could not know the sweet" (D&C 29:39).

In a bone-chilling vision that God gave to Enoch, Enoch saw Satan with a huge chain of darkness veiling the earth (see Moses 7:26). Then the premortal Savior made this sobering declaration:

> Wherefore, I can stretch forth mine hands and hold all the creations which I have made; and mine eye can pierce them also, and among all the workmanship of mine hands there has not been so great wickedness as among thy brethren.
>
> But behold, their sins shall be upon the heads of their fathers; Satan shall be their father, and misery shall be their doom; and the whole heavens shall weep over them, even all the workmanship of mine hands; wherefore should not the heavens weep, seeing these shall suffer? (Moses 7:36–37)

Some believe that the reason this is the wickedest world God ever allowed His spirit children to dwell on is that Satan and his angels were cast to this earth.

When the Lord showed Moses the countless worlds He had made and peopled, Moses's interest was piqued, and he wanted to know more about those worlds. The Lord limited Moses's access to information concerning other worlds by saying,

> But only an account of this earth, and the inhabitants thereof, give I unto you. For behold, there are many worlds that have passed away by the word of my power. And there are many that now stand, and innumerable are they unto man; but all things are numbered unto me, for they are mine and I know them. (Moses 1:35)

Included in that restriction is whether there are evil individuals like Satan on other worlds or whether Satan and his followers who were cast down to this earth can travel to other worlds. All that will be revealed in the Lord's own due time.

In addition to this being the wickedest world, there are specific times on this earth when wickedness is even more prevalent. People living at the time of the Savior were the only people who would be wicked enough to crucify the Savior. Nephi confirms this when he penned Jacob's teaching:

> Wherefore, as I said unto you, it must needs be expedient that Christ—for in the last night the angel spake unto me that this should be his name—should come among the Jews, among those who are the more wicked part of the world; and they shall crucify him—for thus it behooveth our God, and **there is none other nation on earth that would crucify their God.** (2 Nephi 10:3)

We may be inclined to be thankful we were not alive during that wicked generation. However, Joseph Smith said,

> I prophesy, in the name of the Lord God of Israel, anguish and wrath and tribulation and the withdrawing of the Spirit of God from the earth await this generation, until they are visited with utter desolation. **This generation is as corrupt as the generation of the Jews that crucified Christ**; **and if He were here today, and should preach the same doctrine He did then, they would put Him to death**. I defy all the world to destroy the work of God; and I prophesy they never will have power to kill me till my work is accomplished, and I am ready to die. (*Teachings of the Prophet Joseph Smith*, 328)

Even as the premortal Savior wept over those who are overcome by Satan, one may mistakenly believe that we were thrilled to be rid of him and his followers. However, Joseph Smith and Sidney Rigdon saw just the opposite:

> And this we saw also, and bear record, that an **angel of God who was in authority in the presence of God, who rebelled against the Only Begotten Son** whom the Father loved and who was in the bosom of the Father, was thrust down from the presence of God and the Son, And was called Perdition, **for the heavens wept over him—he was Lucifer, a son of the morning.**
>
> And we beheld, and lo, he is fallen! is fallen, even a son of the morning! (D&C 76:25–27)

It is sobering to consider that we, who are here on earth with physical bodies, constituted the "Heavens" mentioned in the above verses. We wept over spirit brothers and sisters who followed Satan. It is not beyond reason to believe that many of our very good friends chose to follow Satan.

It is instructive to note that nowhere in scripture does it refer to "sons of perdition" when referring to Satan and those who followed him in his premortal rebellion. That term "sons of perdition" is reserved for those mortals who "suffer themselves to be overcome" by the devil. That allows for women to follow Satan in his premortal rebellion.

Elder Bruce R. McConkie (1915–1985) gave his apostolic summary of Satan's rebellion and his failed plan:

> When the Eternal Father announced his plan of salvation—a plan that called for a mortal probation for all his spirit children; a plan that required a Redeemer to ransom men from the coming fall; a plan that could only operate if mortal men had agency—when the Father announced his plan, when he chose Christ as the Redeemer and rejected Lucifer, then there was war in heaven. That war was a war of words; it was a conflict of ideologies; it was a rebellion against God and his laws. Lucifer sought to dethrone God, to sit himself on the divine throne, and to save all men without reference to their works. He sought to deny men their agency so they could not sin. He offered a mortal life of carnality and sensuality, of evil and crime and murder, following which all men would be saved. His offer was a philosophical impossibility. There must needs be an opposition in all things. Unless there are opposites, there is nothing. There can be no light without darkness, no heat without cold, no virtue without vice, no good without evil, no salvation without damnation.
>
> And so, in the courts of heaven, the war of wars was waged. Christ and Michael and a mighty host of noble and great spirits preached the gospel of God and exhorted their brethren to follow the Father. Lucifer and his lieutenants preached another gospel, a gospel of fear and hate and lasciviousness and compulsion. They sought salvation without keeping the commandments, without overcoming the world, without choosing between opposites. (McConkie, *The Millennial Messiah* [Salt Lake City: Deseret Book, 1982], 666–67)

Now this former "son of the morning," one who formerly was entrusted with authority of God, completely and forever reversed field and became an enemy to God. Mormon instructed his son, Moroni: "Wherefore, all things which are good cometh of God; and that which is evil cometh of the devil; **for the devil is an enemy unto God, and fighteth against him**

continually, and inviteth and enticeth to sin, and to do that which is evil continually" (Moroni 7:12).

We can and should expect, as Joseph Smith taught, "In relation to the kingdom of God, the devil always sets up his kingdom at the very same time in opposition to God" (*Teachings of the Prophet Joseph Smith*, 365). Carrying that concept to a personal level, whenever you try to do anything that will take you closer to God, you should expect satanic opposition. More will be said of this principle later.

THE PRESENT

Now we shift to Satan's efforts and tactics here in mortality. When his impossible plan to "save all mankind that not one soul would be lost" was rejected, his stated objective changed: "And he became Satan, yea, even the devil, **the father of all lies, to deceive and to blind men, and to lead them captive at his will**, even as many as would not hearken unto my voice" (Moses 4:4).

Since Satan sought to destroy the agency of man in the pre-earth life, we can detect his presence and influence if any substance, activity, or pastime could lead to the forfeiture of our ability to choose. Note the bondage of those addicted to drugs, alcohol, pornography, and so forth. They are as much in bondage as if they were locked up behind steel bars.

Further, it seems that Satan never could comprehend the mind of God with regard to His spirit children. In tempting Eve, Moses saw and recorded: "And Satan put it into the heart of the serpent, (for he had drawn away many after him,) and he sought also to beguile Eve, **for he knew not the mind of God, wherefore he sought to destroy the world**" (Moses 4:6).

Since tempting Eve backfired and resulted in opening the floodgates for the birth of all mankind, Satan must try another tactic. Lehi correctly identified what must have been a serious frustration to Satan: "And after Adam and Eve had partaken of the forbidden fruit they were driven out of the garden of Eden, to till the earth. And they have brought forth children; yea, even the family of all the earth" (2 Nephi 2:19–20).

If Satan couldn't prevent Adam and Eve from having children, he is successfully trying to prevent millions of our Father's spirit children from getting bodies and growing to maturity. How is he doing that? Through convincing men and women that ending a pregnancy is a "right of choice." It is beyond the scope of this book to investigate when the spirit enters the body (it has not yet been revealed), but if the spirit has entered the body, it will have claim upon that body and eventually it will grow to maturity and receive exaltation since all children who die before the age of accountability will receive eternal life (see Mosiah 15:25; D&C 137:10).

Once again Satan's efforts are overcome by the infinite Atonement of Jesus Christ, who provided the avenue by which every son or daughter of Adam and Eve, no matter how long or short they live, will be resurrected. "For as in Adam all die, even so in Christ shall all be made alive" (1 Corinthians 15:22).

It is interesting that the temptation of Eve was not that they could eventually bear children but that they would become like "gods"—the very goal of our Heavenly Father for His spirit children. Remember Moses 1:39: "For behold, this is my work and my glory—to bring to pass the immortality and eternal life of man."

However, the extended account of the temptation of Eve provides a valuable clue for overcoming Satan's temptations. Here is the entire quote that we will draw principles from:

> And he [Satan—see verse 6] said unto the woman:
>
> Yea, hath God said—Ye shall not eat of every tree of the garden? (And he spake by the mouth of the serpent.)
>
> And the woman said unto the serpent: We may eat of the fruit of the trees of the garden;
>
> But of the fruit of the tree which thou beholdest in the midst of the garden, God hath said—Ye shall not eat of it, neither shall ye touch it, lest ye die.
>
> And the serpent said unto the woman: Ye shall not surely die;
> For God doth know that in the day ye eat thereof, then your eyes shall be opened, and ye shall be as gods, knowing good and evil.
>
> And when the woman saw that the tree was good for food, and that it became pleasant to the eyes, and a tree to be desired to make her wise, she took of the fruit thereof, and did eat, and also gave unto her husband with her, and he did eat. (Moses 4:6–12)

First, Satan tried to determine if God had forbidden any activity. Naively—or more accurately—"innocently," the woman said they could eat of all the fruits in the Garden of Eden. Then, being perfectly honest, she noticed the fruit of the Tree of Knowledge of Good and Evil that the Lord had forbidden them to eat.

Satan seems to say to himself, "I have my mark!" Next, he contradicts God's stated consequences for disobeying His command: "Ye shall not surely die" and then added that most desirable goal—one which he could have obtained but because of his rebellion forfeited forever—to be like gods.

It is interesting to note the location of the Tree of Knowledge of Good and Evil that bore the forbidden fruit. It wasn't secreted in some obscure corner of the Garden where they would never see it, but was in the midst—a place where they likely passed every day. Now the next part gives us one important key to avoiding Satan's temptations. It wasn't until Satan successfully tempted Eve to focus her attention on the forbidden fruit that it "became pleasant to the eye, a tree to be desired."

If we could follow the Savior's example of not giving Satan the time of day, he would never be able to tempt us to do evil. "For the prince of this world cometh, and hath nothing in me" (John 14:30).

James reiterated that same principle when he taught, "Submit yourselves therefore to God. **Resist the devil, and he will flee from you**" (James 4:7).

It didn't take Satan long to contradict the teachings of Adam and Eve as they sought to help their children understand the great plan of salvation. Moses records,

> And Adam and Eve blessed the name of God, and they made all things known unto their sons and their daughters.
>
> And Satan came among them, saying: I am also a son of God; and he commanded them, saying: **Believe it not; and they believed it not, and they loved Satan more than God**. And men began from that time forth to be carnal, sensual, and devilish. (Moses 5:12–13)

God has ordained prophets from the days of Adam to our day whenever there have been a people who would listen to them as they taught the Father's plan of salvation. Following the prophets leads to safety and protection. Disobeying their counsel leads to captivity and destruction. When John the Revelator saw our day, he wrote in unmistakable language what Satan would do and the reason behind it.

> And I heard a loud voice saying in heaven, Now is come salvation, and strength, and the kingdom of our God, and the power of his Christ: for **the accuser of our brethren is cast down, which accused them before our God day and night.**
>
> And they overcame him by the blood of the Lamb, and by the word of their testimony; and they loved not their lives unto the death.

> Therefore rejoice, *ye* heavens, and ye that dwell in them. Woe to the inhabiters of the earth and of the sea! **for the devil is come down unto you, having great wrath, because he knoweth that he hath but a short time.** (Revelation 12:10–12)

Satan has always deceived people into believing that prophets had to be sinless in order to qualify to speak for God. Such was the case in the days of the apostles. James refuted that false idea by teaching, "Elias was a man subject to like passions as we are, and he prayed earnestly that it might not rain: and it rained not on the earth by the space of three years and six months. And he prayed again, and the heaven gave rain, and the earth brought forth her fruit" (James 5:17–18).

Even today there are members of the Church who revel in pointing out the flaws or weaknesses of those the Lord has chosen to lead us during these perilous times. Truly Isaiah saw our day when he said of those who undermine our confidence in our leaders because of a misspoken word: "For the terrible one is brought to nought, and the scorner is consumed, and **all that watch for iniquity are cut off: That make a man an offender for a word, and lay a snare for him that reproveth in the gate, and turn aside the just for a thing of nought"** (Isaiah 29:20–21).

Many of the ancient apostles raised a warning voice to our generation knowing that the prophesied apostasy would deprive many from embracing the teaching of living prophets. Peter said, "Be sober, be vigilant; because your adversary the devil, as a roaring lion, walketh about, seeking whom he may devour" (1 Peter 5:8).

Nephi was concerned about our day as we approach the Second Coming. He enlarged upon what we mentioned earlier about there being no devil. He describes his tactics which should act as a warning to us:

> For the kingdom of the devil must shake, and they which belong to it must needs be stirred up unto repentance, or the devil will grasp them with his everlasting chains, and **they be stirred up to anger, and perish**;
>
> For behold, at that day **shall he rage in the hearts of the children of men, and stir them up to anger against that which is good.**
>
> And **others will he pacify, and lull them away into carnal security**, that they will say: All is well in Zion; yea, Zion prospereth, all is well—and **thus the devil cheateth their souls, and leadeth them away carefully down to hell.**
>
> And behold, **others he flattereth away, and telleth them there is no hell; and he saith unto them: I am no devil, for there is none**—and

> thus he whispereth in their ears, until he grasps them with his awful chains, from whence there is no deliverance. (2 Nephi 28:19–22)

It is interesting to note that Satan uses the entire spectrum of emotions to deceive and destroy people. From filling people with rage and anger against anything that is good, to lullabying people into Satan-induced apathy where they refuse to get involved in a good cause, choosing to sit on the sidelines and "sip soda."

One need only listen to the news on the radio or watch television broadcasts to see the number of incidents of road rage, domestic violence, gang shootings, and so on. On the one hand, people seem to be infuriated at the least provocation. On the other hand is complacency about world conditions and domestic violence that promotes the "all is well in Zion" attitude. Nephi couldn't have described our day more accurately, and he did it over 2600 years ago.

For those who doubt that the Book of Mormon prophets saw our day, a careful reading of the following verses should dispel all doubt:

> For it [secret combinations] cometh to pass that whoso buildeth it up **seeketh to overthrow the freedom of all lands, nations, and countries; and it bringeth to pass the destruction of all people, for it is built up by the devil**, who is the father of all lies; even that same liar who beguiled our first parents, yea, even that same liar who hath caused man to commit murder from the beginning; who hath hardened the hearts of men that they have murdered the prophets, and stoned them, and cast them out from the beginning. (Ether 8:25)

Moroni, the last surviving Nephite prophet, penned that warning as he was abridging the record of the Jaredites who allowed the secret combinations to go unchecked. He had also watched as those same secret combinations completely destroyed his people.

Mormon had written about the rise and fall of the Nephite nation, which preceded the first coming of Christ. He identified the source of all the wickedness that eventually led to their destruction:

> Now behold, those secret oaths and covenants did not come forth unto Gadianton from the records which were delivered unto Helaman; but behold, **they were put into the heart of Gadianton by that same being who did entice our first parents to partake of the forbidden fruit—**

> Yea, that **same being who did plot with Cain**, that if he would murder his brother Abel it should not be known unto the world. And he did plot with Cain and his followers from that time forth.
>
> And also it is that same being who **put it into the hearts of the people to build a tower sufficiently high that they might get to heaven**. And it was that same being who led on the people who came from that tower into this land; who **spread the works of darkness and abominations over all the face of the land**, until he dragged the people down to an entire destruction, and to an everlasting hell.
>
> Yea, it is that same being who put it into the heart of Gadianton to still carry on the work of darkness, and of secret murder; and he has brought it forth from the beginning of man even down to this time.
>
> And behold, **it is he who is the author of all sin**. And behold, he doth carry on his works of darkness and secret murder, and **doth hand down their plots, and their oaths, and their covenants, and their plans of awful wickedness, from generation to generation** according as he can get hold upon the hearts of the children of men. (Helaman 6:26–30; for additional tactics read D&C 10:12–28)

Even within the Church, among strong members, Satan uses a clever tactic to deprive us of enjoying the Spirit:

> And this I do that I may establish my gospel, that there may not be so much contention; yea, **Satan doth stir up the hearts of the people to contention concerning the points of my doctrine**; and in these things they do err, for they do wrest the scriptures and do not understand them. (D&C 10:63)

What is the harm in flirting with the devil just a little? He certainly has the ability to make sin look fun and exciting. However, even Adam discovered the problem with taking just that first step into Satan's territory:

> Wherefore, it came to pass that the devil tempted **Adam**, and he partook of the forbidden fruit and transgressed the commandment, **wherein he became subject to the will of the devil, because he yielded unto temptation.** (D&C 29:39–40)

President George Albert Smith taught,

> A good man who was a counselor to President Brigham Young said upon one occasion, "There is a **line of demarcation well defined**. On one side of the line is the Lord's territory, and on the other side of the line

> is the devil's territory. If you will stay on the Lord's side of the line, the devil cannot come over there to tempt you or to annoy or distress you. If you go onto the devil's side of the line just one inch, you are in his territory, you are in his power, and he will seek to draw you just as far from that line of demarcation, that division line, as he can, knowing that if he can keep you in his territory he has you in his power." (Conference Report, October 1932, 27)

At times, we members of the Church feel as though we have a target on our backs where the devils take aim. That isn't so wrong! You might remember what the Lord revealed in D&C 29:39: "And it must needs be that the devil should tempt **the children of men**." The Lord differentiated between "the children of men" (people who were not members of the Church) and the "saints of God" or "the sons of God" (see Moses 8:13–14). Although the devil "tempts" the children of men, "**he maketh war with the saints of God, and encompasseth them round about"** (D&C 76:29). This will be discussed later in this book.

It is easy to see the difference between "tempting" and "making war by encompassing round about." Joseph Smith will enlarge upon this subject later in this book.

There seems to be varying degrees of Satan's influence on people. First, he "tempts." At that point, they have the power to resist. Joseph Smith taught, "All beings who have bodies have power over those who have not. The devil has no power over us only as we permit him. The moment we revolt at anything which comes from God, the devil takes power" (*Teachings of the Prophet Joseph Smith*, 181).

It would be a mistake to assume that everything mankind does that is contrary to Heavenly Father's will is a direct result of Satan's temptation. Joseph Smith further enlightened us:

> He then observed that Satan was generally blamed for the evils which we did, but if he was the cause of all our wickedness, men could not be condemned. The devil could not compel mankind to do evil; all was voluntary. Those who resisted the Spirit of God, would be liable to be led into temptation, and then the association of heaven would be withdrawn from those who refused to be made partakers of such great glory. God would not exert any compulsory means, and the devil could not; and such ideas as were entertained [on these subjects] by many were absurd. (*Teachings of the Prophet Joseph Smith*, 187)

Keeping our focus upward and on eternal life helps us avoid the clever temptations of the adversary. In a revelation following a rather comprehensive revelation concerning the Second Coming (see D&C 45), the Lord revealed,

> But ye are commanded in all things to ask of God, who giveth liberally; and that which the Spirit testifies unto you even so I would that ye should do in all holiness of heart, walking uprightly before me, considering the end of your salvation, doing all things with prayer and thanksgiving, that ye may not be seduced by evil spirits, or doctrines of devils, or the commandments of men; for some are of men, and others of devils. (D&C 46:7)

Those spiritual gifts mentioned in D&C 46, Moroni 10, and 1 Corinthians 11 provide a partial list of resources necessary to detect and overcome the subtle temptations of the devils that surround us.

Satan has great power. Unless we understand what he can and cannot do, we put ourselves in harm's way. Paul warned, "And no marvel; for Satan himself is transformed into an angel of light" (2 Corinthians 11:14).

The Savior graciously revealed to Joseph Smith the keys for detecting Satan if he appears as an angel of light.

> If he be the spirit of a just man made perfect he will come in his glory; for that is the only way he can appear—
>
> Ask him to shake hands with you, but he will not move, because it is contrary to the order of heaven for a just man to deceive; but he will still deliver his message.
>
> **If it be the devil as an angel of light, when you ask him to shake hands he will offer you his hand, and you will not feel anything; you may therefore detect him.** (D&C 129:6–8)

There is yet another quote by Joseph Smith that may help us detect Satan as he attempts to deceive and destroy us: "**Why will the devil comply if he knows he will be detected?** 'The **Devil . . . will either shrink back . . . or offer his hand**.' He will not remain absolutely still if he is tested" (*The Words of Joseph Smith, The Contemporary Accounts of the Nauvoo Discourses of the Prophet Joseph*, edited by Andrew F. Ehat and Lyndon W. Cook, Religious Studies [Salt Lake City: Bookcraft, 1980], 20–21; see also rsc.byu.edu/words-joseph-smith/december-1840).

In our quest to qualify for eternal life, we would do well to discover how God governs His spirit children in the heavens, and then try to implement those same principles here on earth. In D&C 121:34–36, the Lord warns us of two of Satan's diversionary tactics that retard our progress toward eternal life.

> Behold, there are many called, but few are chosen. And why are they not chosen?
>
> [1] Because their hearts are set so much upon the things of this world, and [2] aspire to the honors of men, that they do not learn this one lesson—
>
> That the rights of the priesthood are inseparably connected with the powers of heaven, and that **the powers of heaven cannot be controlled nor handled only upon the principles of righteousness.**

A few verses later, the Lord outlines what those principles of righteousness are

> No power or influence can or ought to be maintained by virtue of the priesthood, only by persuasion, by long-suffering, by gentleness and meekness, and by love unfeigned; By kindness, and pure knowledge, which shall greatly enlarge the soul without hypocrisy, and without guile—
>
> Reproving betimes with sharpness, when moved upon by the Holy Ghost; and then showing forth afterwards an increase of love toward him whom thou hast reproved, lest he esteem thee to be his enemy;
>
> That he may know that thy faithfulness is stronger than the cords of death.
>
> Let thy bowels also be full of charity towards all men, and to the household of faith, and let virtue garnish thy thoughts unceasingly. (D&C 121:41–45)

One year while I was preparing to teach this section of the Doctrine and Covenants to the students at BYU, I considered each of the eleven principles of righteousness. I may have been overly confident that I was doing a pretty good job myself of living by them. But remembering that the devil always sets up his kingdom in direct opposition to God's kingdom, I decided to consult a thesaurus to see what the antonyms of those words are. Below is a chart that clearly revealed that although I was making progress in applying the principles of righteousness, I had a lot of work to do to eliminate Satan's opposite attributes. See if you discover the same thing.

11 Principles of Righteousness and Their Opposites D&C 121:41–45

GODLY PRINCIPLE	SATAN'S OPPOSING INFLUENCE
1) **Persuasion**	Force, duress, pressure, demanding, guilt trip
2) **Long-suffering**	Short fuse, intolerant, quick to anger, impatient, insistent, irritable, mean, always have to be right, stubborn, close-minded
3) **Gentleness and meekness**	Violence, defiance, mean-spirited, antagonistic, contentious
4) **Love unfeigned**	Forced affection, alienation, isolation, hatred
5) **Kindness**	Anger, cruelty, miserliness
6) **Pure knowledge, which shall enlarge the soul without hypocrisy**	Closed-mindedness, false traditions, incorrect theories, false ideas, lack of understanding
7) **Without guile**	Trickery, deceit, insincerity, lack of honesty in dealings
8) **Reproving betimes with sharpness when moved upon by the Holy Ghost**	Global anger, non-specific castigations, dredging up past, ungodly anger, rage, false accusations
9) **Showing forth afterwards an increase of love toward him whom thou has reproved, lest he esteem thee to be his enemy**	Withholding affections, continuing to punish, sulking, unwillingness to communicate, moodiness, irritability, melancholy, oppressiveness, pessimism

10) Let thy bowels also be full of charity towards all men, and to the Household of faith (D&C 88:125—charity is the bond of perfectness and peace)	Tearing down, putting down, condescending remarks, agitation, combative
11) Let virtue garnish thy thoughts unceasingly	Immoral, low, course, evil, fault-finding, worthlessness, imperfections, ineffectiveness

Before leaving Satan in the present and considering what lies ahead for him and his followers, as you read the scriptures, you may want to take the challenge to note those attributes the Savior commands us to live by and see the opposite influences Satan and his followers try to lure us into incorporating into our way of interfacing with each other.

Let us not forget that first, last, and always, the purpose for Christ's coming in addition to working out the infinite Atonement: "He that committeth sin is of the devil; for the devil sinneth from the beginning. **For this purpose the Son of God was manifested, that he might destroy the works of the devil**" (1 John 3:8).

THE FUTURE

Satan has a dwindling number of days before he is confined to a prison house for a thousand years and then loosed for a little season before being banished to outer darkness forever. The Savior begins this part of our study by stating,

> I AM Alpha and Omega, Christ the Lord; yea, even I am he, the beginning and the end, the Redeemer of the world.
>
> I, having accomplished and finished the will of him whose I am, even the Father, concerning me—having done this that I might subdue all things unto myself—
>
> Retaining all power, even to **the destroying of Satan and his works at the end of the world, and the last great day of judgment**, which I shall pass upon the inhabitants thereof, judging every man according to his works and the deeds which he hath done. (D&C 19:1–3)

The Lord defines "the end of the world" as, "And what is the sign of thy coming, and of the **end of the world**, or the *destruction of the wicked*, which is the **end of the world**?" (Joseph Smith—Matthew 1:4). That happens at the beginning of the Millennium. The "end of the earth" comes over a thousand years later. "And these are the rest of the dead; and they live not again until the *thousand years are ended*, neither again, until the **end of the earth**" (D&C 88:101).

Until the beginning of the Millennium, Satan and his followers will intensify their efforts to destroy, to make mankind "miserable like unto themselves" (2 Nephi 2:18, 27). He will stir them up to iniquity against that which is good (D&C 10:20). He will constantly stir people up and make them angry one against another in his hellish attempt to lead their souls to destruction (D&C 10:21–22). "Yea, he stirreth up their hearts to anger against this work" (D&C 10:24). Opposition to the gospel and those who are spreading the gospel will continue to intensify. He will encourage lying and deceit. He will use flattery and cause people to catch themselves in their own lies (see D&C 10:25–28).

When the Millennium is ushered in by the Savior's return, Satan will have no more power over those who are not destroyed.

> For a desolating scourge shall go forth among the inhabitants of the earth, and shall continue to be poured out from time to time, if they repent not, until the earth is empty, and the inhabitants thereof are consumed away and utterly destroyed by the brightness of my coming. (D&C 5:19)
>
> For the great Millennium, of which I have spoken by the mouth of my servants, shall come.
>
> For Satan shall be bound, and when he is loosed again he shall only reign for a little season, and then cometh the end of the earth. (D&C 43:30–31)

The Savior is very definite that Satan will have some kind of restraint put on him that will prevent him from tempting people during the Millennium. "And Satan shall be bound, that he shall have no place in the hearts of the children of men" (D&C 45:55).

There seems to be at least three ways that Satan will be bound during the Millennium:

(1) By the destruction of the wicked who now empower him by their wicked deeds.

> For behold, saith the prophet, the time cometh speedily that Satan shall have no more power over the hearts of the children of men; for the day soon cometh that **all the proud and they who do wickedly shall be as stubble; and the day cometh that they must be burned.** (1 Nephi 22:15)

(2) He will be bound by the righteousness of the people who remain after the destruction of the wicked.

> And **because of the righteousness of his people, Satan has no power**; wherefore, he cannot be loosed for the space of many years; for he hath no power over the hearts of the people, for they dwell in righteousness, and the Holy One of Israel reigneth. (1 Nephi 22:26)

(3) There will be some kind of physical restraint put on him by the Lord.

> And so on, until the seventh angel shall sound his trump; and he shall stand forth upon the land and upon the sea, and swear in the name of him who sitteth upon the throne, that there shall be time no longer; and **Satan shall be bound**, that old serpent, who is called the devil, and shall not be loosed for the space of a thousand years. (D&C 88:110)

During that thousand-year period, because Satan has no power to tempt, the Lord affirms, "And the earth shall be given unto them for an inheritance; and they shall multiply and wax strong, and their children shall grow up without sin unto salvation" (D&C 45:58).

Enmity or the natural hatred, of which Satan seems to be the author, will cease. The Lord says, "And in that day the enmity of man, and the enmity of beasts, yea, the **enmity of all flesh**, *shall cease* from before my face" (D&C 101:26).

Isaiah saw the Millennial day and described it in these words:

> The wolf also shall dwell with the lamb, and the leopard shall lie down with the kid; and the calf and the young lion and the fatling together; and a little child shall lead them.
>
> And the cow and the bear shall feed; their young ones shall lie down together: and the lion shall eat straw like the ox.
>
> And the sucking child shall play on the hole of the asp, and the weaned child shall put his hand on the cockatrice' den.

> They shall not hurt nor destroy in all my holy mountain: for the earth shall be full of the knowledge of the LORD, as the waters cover the sea. (Isaiah 11:6–9)

The Savior enlarges upon the millennial condition as He reveals,

> And in that day all who are found upon the watch-tower, or in other words, all mine Israel, shall be saved.
>
> And they that have been scattered shall be gathered.
>
> And all they who have mourned shall be comforted.
>
> And all they who have given their lives for my name shall be crowned.
>
> Therefore, let your hearts be comforted concerning Zion; for all flesh is in mine hands; be still and know that I am God. (D&C 101:12–16)

The description of the millennial day almost defies comprehension. The Lord revealed,

> And in that day whatsoever any man shall ask, it shall be given unto him.
>
> And in that day Satan shall not have power to tempt any man.
>
> And there shall be no sorrow because there is no death.
>
> In that day an infant shall not die until he is old; and his life shall be as the age of a tree;
>
> And when he dies he shall not sleep, that is to say in the earth, but shall be changed in the twinkling of an eye, and shall be caught up, and his rest shall be glorious.
>
> Yea, verily I say unto you, in that day when the Lord shall come, he shall reveal all things—
>
> Things which have passed, and hidden things which no man knew, things of the earth, by which it was made, and the purpose and the end thereof—
>
> Things most precious, things that are above, and things that are beneath, things that are in the earth, and upon the earth, and in heaven.
>
> And all they who suffer persecution for my name, and endure in faith, though they are called to lay down their lives for my sake yet shall they partake of all this glory.

> Wherefore, fear not even unto death; for in this world your joy is not full, but in me your joy is full. (D&C 101:27–36)

Given that heavenly condition, with Christ dwelling amongst the Saints, it is difficult to envision why anyone would want to sin. "For I will reveal myself from heaven with power and great glory, with all the hosts thereof, and dwell in righteousness with men on earth a thousand years, and the wicked shall not stand" (D&C 29:11).

However, the scriptures attest that toward the end of the Millennium, "And again, verily, verily, I say unto you that when the thousand years are ended, and **men again begin to deny their God,** then will I spare the earth but for a little season" (D&C 29:22).

As the wickedness of mortals then living on the earth increases, Satan is loosed. John, the Revelator saw the end and recorded it in these words:

> And when the thousand years are expired, **Satan shall be loosed out of his prison,**
>
> **And shall go out to deceive the nations** which are in the four quarters of the earth, Gog and Magog, **to gather them together to battle**: the number of whom *is* as the sand of the sea.
>
> And they went up on the breadth of the earth, and compassed the camp of the saints about, and the beloved city: and fire came down from God out of heaven, and devoured them.
>
> And the devil that deceived them was cast into the lake of fire and brimstone, where the beast and the false prophet *are,* and shall be tormented day and night for ever and ever. (Revelation 20:7–10)

So important is the final battle between God and Satan that the Lord revealed more details to the Prophet Joseph Smith:

> And then he shall be loosed for a little season, that he may gather together his armies.
>
> And Michael, the seventh angel, even the archangel, shall gather together his armies, even the hosts of heaven.
>
> And the devil shall gather together his armies; even the hosts of hell, and shall come up to battle against Michael and his armies.
>
> And then cometh **the battle of the great God**; and the devil and his armies shall be cast away into their own place, that they shall not have power over the saints any more at all.

> For Michael shall fight their battles, and shall overcome him who seeketh the throne of him who sitteth upon the throne, even the Lamb. (D&C 88:111–115)

The battle of Gog and Magog (as named in the book of Revelation) is called "The battle of the great God" in the Doctrine and Covenants.

Since the Lord knows "the end from the beginning" (see Abraham 2:8), He has made a place or accommodation for Satan and his followers: "And they were thrust down, and thus came the devil and his angels; And, behold, there is a place prepared for them from the beginning, which place is hell" (D&C 29:37–38).

The full extent of the conditions in outer darkness are reserved for those who are consigned to that punishment. Of those mortals who allow themselves to be overcome after having embraced the fullness of the gospel, the Lord revealed,

> They are they who are the sons of perdition, of whom I say that it had been better for them never to have been born;
>
> For they are vessels of wrath, doomed to suffer the wrath of God, with the devil and his angels in eternity;
>
> Concerning whom I have said there is no forgiveness in this world nor in the world to come—
>
> Having denied the Holy Spirit after having received it, and having denied the Only Begotten Son of the Father, having crucified him unto themselves and put him to an open shame.
>
> These are they who shall go away into the lake of fire and brimstone, with the devil and his angels—
>
> And the only ones on whom the second death shall have any power. (D&C 76:32–37)

Further describing their condition, the Lord revealed,

> Who glorifies the Father, and saves all the works of his hands, except those sons of perdition who deny the Son after the Father has revealed him.
>
> Wherefore, he saves all except them—they shall go away into everlasting punishment, which is endless punishment, which is eternal punishment, **to reign with the devil and his angels in eternity,** where their worm dieth not, and the fire is not quenched, which is their torment—

> And the end thereof, neither the place thereof, nor their torment, no man knows;
>
> Neither was it revealed, neither is, neither will be revealed unto man, except to them who are made partakers thereof;
>
> Nevertheless, I, the Lord, show it by vision unto many, but straightway shut it up again;
>
> Wherefore, the end, the width, the height, the depth, and the misery thereof, they understand not, neither any man except those who are ordained [sentenced or consigned] unto this condemnation. (D&C 76:43–48)

Alma saw the final end of the sons of perdition and wrote,

> Then is the time when their torments shall be as a lake of fire and brimstone, whose flame ascendeth up forever and ever; and then is the time that they shall be chained down to an everlasting destruction, according to the power and captivity of Satan, he having subjected them according to his will.
>
> Then, I say unto you, they shall be as though there had been no redemption made; for they cannot be redeemed according to God's justice; and they cannot die, seeing there is no more corruption. (Alma 12:17–18)

As the Lord described the glory of those spirit children who will inherit the different degrees of glory according to the law that they lived (see D&C 88:21–24), He also recorded the choice and fate of the sons of perdition:

> Ye who are quickened by a portion of the celestial glory shall then receive of the same, even a fulness.
>
> And they who are quickened by a portion of the terrestrial glory shall then receive of the same, even a fulness.
>
> And also they who are quickened by a portion of the telestial glory shall then receive of the same, even a fulness.
>
> And they who remain shall also be quickened; nevertheless, they shall return again to their own place, **to enjoy that which they are willing to receive, because they were not willing to enjoy that which they might have received.** (D&C 88:29–32)

Those who were faithful enough to follow Christ in the pre-earth life, embraced the gospel and the ordinances—including the priesthood—here on earth, and then allowed themselves to be overcome by the temptations of Satan will go to the place where they will "enjoy" what they were willing to receive, because they were not willing to "enjoy" exaltation, which they might have received.

One can only hope that relatively few mortals will ever become sons of perdition—perdition meaning utterly worthless and totally ruined.

Concerning that spirit brother who could have enjoyed eternal life and exaltation with God and Christ, who exercised his agency not only to rebel and incite a mutiny against God, but also used his charismatic influence to lead one third part of our Father's children away to eternal destruction, we can only hope and pray that we are wise enough to avoid his merciless, relentless attacks on us with his sole objective of dragging us down to an endless hell to be miserable like unto himself.

CHAPTER 2

Christ Is the Key to Success

Over more than four decades of counseling with people struggling with the challenges of mortality, especially those trying to escape the monsters of addiction, one thing has become abundantly clear: without additional help, frequent relapses are more prevalent than successes.

Why is that so? In searching for a solution that works, I found, in a most unlikely place, the problem and the solution. When the ancient prophet-historian Mormon was compiling what would become the Book of Mormon, he was explaining the transition from the kings to the judges. Look carefully at his insightful analysis.

First, can we agree that anyone who is addicted to a substance, a practice, or a habit is in bondage? If we agree, here is Mormon's prophetic solution:

> Behold what great destruction did come upon them; and also because of their iniquities they were brought into bondage.
>
> And **were it not for the interposition of their all-wise Creator**, and this because of their sincere repentance, **they must unavoidably remain in bondage until now.**
>
> But behold, he did deliver them because they did humble themselves before him; and because they cried mightily unto him he did deliver them out of bondage; and **thus doth the Lord work with his power in all cases among the children of men**, extending the arm of mercy towards them that put their trust in him. (Mosiah 29:18–20)

It is obvious that if a person never took the first drink, he would never become an alcoholic. If he had never experimented with drugs, he would never become a drug addict. If he never viewed pornography the first time, he would never have to fight the endless war trying to break the habit. So, as Mormon noted, it was "because of their iniquities" that they become addicted.

That is a great observation, but it isn't particularly helpful to those who are currently struggling to overcome evil. However, the next point Mormon makes holds the first, last, and only sure solution to retaking control of our lives. "And **were it not for the interposition of their all-wise Creator**, . . . **they must unavoidably remain in bondage until now.**"

"Interposition" means to stand between two opposing or antagonistic foes. Christ, the "all-wise Creator" said the same thing when He was ministering among the Jewish people. "I am the vine, ye *are* the branches: He that abideth in me, and I in him, the same bringeth forth much fruit: for **without me ye can do nothing**" (John 15:5).

Let's consider the parts of Mormon's formula to get Christ to "interpose" on our behalf. First was "**sincere repentance**." It is impossible for one to listen to general conference since President Russell M. Nelson has become prophet to miss the frequent calls to repent.

The Bible dictionary defines "repentance" as "a change of mind, i.e., a fresh view about God, about oneself, and about the world." Further the dictionary states: "Repentance comes to mean a turning of the heart and will to God, and a renunciation of sin to which we are naturally inclined" (Bible Dictionary, 760).

Mormon's use of the word "sincere" suggests that our desire to change must be genuine and complete. James confirmed that when he wrote, "A double minded man is unstable in all his ways" (James 1:8). That observation was preceded by his counsel: "For let not that man think that he shall receive anything of the Lord" (James 1:7).

How long before the Lord will "interpose" on our behalf? Amulek gives the answer:

> Yea, I would that ye would come forth and harden not your hearts any longer; for behold, now is the time and the day of your salvation; and therefore, if ye will repent and harden not your hearts, **immediately** shall the great plan of redemption be brought about unto you. (Alma 34:31)

The end result (such as completely and permanently overcoming our addictions) may be yet future, but the first step and the divine help happen immediately.

The next part of Mormon's formula is, "Because they did **humble** themselves before him." James seems to be having a conversation with

Mormon. He wrote, "But he giveth more grace. Wherefore he saith, **God resisteth the proud, but giveth grace unto the humble**. Submit yourselves therefore to God. Resist the devil, and he will flee from you" (James 4:6–7).

Remember that grace is a "divine enabling power." It is the power necessary to win the war against Satan and his followers.

The great King Solomon joined the conversation between Mormon and James when he said, "These six *things* doth the LORD hate: yea, seven *are* an abomination unto him: **A proud look** . . ." (Proverbs 6:16–17). The other six things are listed but not pertinent to our present discussion. *Webster's New World Dictionary* defines "humility" as "a state or quality of being humble; absence of pride or self-assertion" (4th edition [New York City: Simon & Schuster/Pocket Books, 2003]).

Next Mormon states, "And because **they cried mightily unto him**." Prayer is our lifeline to God. The Lord revealed to Joseph Smith this vital key in overcoming Satan and avoiding those who care more for money than for the souls of men. "Pray always, that you may come off conqueror; yea, that you may conquer Satan, and that you may escape the hands of the servants of Satan that do uphold his work" (D&C 10:5). What is Satan's work? "For he [Satan] knew not the mind of God, wherefore he sought to destroy the world" (Moses 4:6). Establishing a regular, frequent, sincere prayer regimen focuses our mind on God and eternal things rather than on the roadblocks Satan throws in our way.

Finally Mormon states, "[that God] extend[s His] arm of mercy towards them that put their trust in him." Believing that God can and will help you overcome any and all undesirable habits or practices is essential in triggering His divine help. So all-inclusive is His promise that Mormon states, "And thus doth the Lord work with his power **in all cases** among the children of men."

Is it any wonder that the Lord instructed and encouraged His Saints to "Look unto me in every thought; doubt not, fear not"? (D&C 6:36).

CHAPTER 3

Start Taking Control NOW—Game On!

From ancient times, the Lord has shown prophets what world conditions would be as the time of the Second Coming approaches. In a bone-chilling vision, the premortal Savior showed Enoch the conditions we are currently experiencing.

> And he saw angels descending out of heaven; and he heard a loud voice saying: Wo, wo be unto the inhabitants of the earth.
>
> And he beheld Satan; and he had a great chain in his hand, and it veiled the whole face of the earth with darkness; and he looked up and laughed, and his angels rejoiced. (Moses 7:25–26)

Isaiah confirmed Enoch's vision but also gave us some hope:

> ARISE, shine; for thy light is come, and the glory of the LORD is risen upon thee.
>
> For, behold, the darkness shall cover the earth, and gross darkness the people: but the LORD shall arise upon thee, and his glory shall be seen upon thee. (Isaiah 60:1–2)

Through the Prophet Joseph Smith, the Lord explained the sequence of His planned destruction in the latter days:

> Verily, verily, I say unto you, darkness covereth the earth, and gross darkness the minds of the people, and all flesh has become corrupt before my face.

> Behold, vengeance cometh speedily upon the inhabitants of the earth, a day of wrath, a day of burning, a day of desolation, of weeping, of mourning, and of lamentation; and as a whirlwind it shall come upon all the face of the earth, saith the Lord.
>
> And upon my house shall it begin, and from my house shall it go forth, saith the Lord;
>
> First among those among you, saith the Lord, who have professed to know my name and have not known me, and have blasphemed against me in the midst of my house, saith the Lord. (D&C 112:23–26)

Joseph Smith lamented the conditions in his day—and it is obvious things haven't improved since.

> For some length of time I have been carefully viewing the state of things, as it now appears, throughout our Christian land; and have looked at it with feelings of the most painful anxiety. While upon one hand I behold the manifest withdrawal of God's Holy Spirit, and the **veil of stupidity** which seems to be drawn over the hearts of the people; upon the other hand, I behold the judgments of God that have swept, and are still sweeping hundreds and thousands of our race, and I fear unprepared, down to the shades of death. With this solemn and alarming fact before me, I am led to exclaim, "O that my head were waters, and mine eyes a fountain of tears, that I might weep day and night." (*Teachings of the Prophet Joseph Smith*, 13–14)

Given the darkness that covers the earth and the gross darkness that clouds the minds of the masses, how are we to survive the days ahead? First, we must see the battle for what it is. Unless we acknowledge that we are in the mists of a battle with Satan for the souls of men, we underestimate the magnitude of the challenge. Brigham Young taught,

> I wish my brethren and sisters to understand that the contest between themselves and the power of Satan is now, to-day, and has been ever since the Lord Almighty bestowed his Holy Priesthood upon his servant Joseph. When holy angels were sent from heaven to call and ordain Joseph Smith, and he to ordain others, the war commenced against sin and the power of it, and will continue until the earth shall be cleansed from it, and shall be made a fit habitation for Saints and angels. The Holy Priesthood has been restored expressly for this purpose. **There is nothing that the Saints can ask, or pray for, that will aid them in their progress to the attainment of all the freedom, liberty, power, and conquest, that they are capable**

of desiring and making a good use of, that will not be granted unto them, if they will only patiently struggle on. I am happy in saying that the Lord is doing his work most admirably. Are we progressing as fast as the work of the Lord is progressing? He has pled with the people by the voice of his Spirit, by the voice of angels, and by the voice of his servants; but their ears are heavy. He is pleading now with the sword, as well as with the voice of his servants, and he will plead with them by tempest and storm, and soon will plead with them by famine and by pestilence. The Savior has said: "And ye shall hear of wars, and rumors of wars; see that ye be not troubled; for all these things must come to pass, but the end is not yet. For nation shall rise against nation, and kingdom against kingdom; and there shall be famines, and pestilences and earthquakes in divers places. All these are the beginning of sorrows."

The men and women, who desire to obtain seats in the celestial kingdom, will find that they must battle with the enemy of all righteousness every day. "Stand therefore, having your loins girt about with truth, and having on the breastplate of righteousness; and your feet shod with the preparation of the Gospel of peace; above all, taking the shield of faith, wherewith ye shall be able to quench all the fiery darts of the wicked. And take the helmet of salvation, and the sword of the Spirit, which is the word of God; praying always with all prayer and supplication in the spirit, and watching there unto with all perseverance and supplication for all Saints." **Thus let every Saint protect and guard his little castle against every effort of the enemy to assail, and secure a foothold therein. Let us see to it that we are ready for the enemy, to baffle him at every point, contending bravely against him until he is successfully repulsed.** (*Journal of Discourses*, 26 vols. [London: Latter-day Saints' Book Depot, 1854–86], 11:14)

We have recently been warned that persecution may follow us. Joseph Smith prophetically outlined what is happening to us:

The enemies of this people will never get weary of their persecution against the Church, until they are overcome. I expect they will array everything against me [and you!] that is in their power to control, and that we shall have a long and tremendous warfare. He that will war the true Christian warfare against the corruptions of these last days will have wicked men and angels of devils, and all the infernal powers of darkness continually arrayed against him. **When wicked and corrupt men oppose, it is a criterion to judge if a man is warring the Christian warfare.** When all men speak evil of you falsely, blessed are ye. Shall a man be considered bad, when men speak evil of him? No. If a man stands and opposes the world of sin, he may expect to have all wicked

> and corrupt spirits arrayed against him. But it will be but a little season, and all these afflictions will be turned away from us, inasmuch as we are faithful, and are not overcome by these evils. By seeing the blessings of the endowment rolling on, and the kingdom increasing and spreading from sea to sea, we shall rejoice that we were not overcome by these foolish things. (*Teachings of the Prophet Joseph Smith*, 259)

Many have asked why we are bombarded with so much temptation, persecution, and trials. Brigham Young taught,

> I ask, is there a reason for men and women being exposed more constantly and more powerfully, to the power of the enemy, by having visions than by not having them? There is and it is simply this—God never bestows upon His people, or upon an individual, superior blessings without a severe trial to prove them, to prove that individual, or that people to see whether they will keep their covenants with him, and keep in remembrance what He has shown them. Then the greater the vision, the greater the display of the power of the enemy. And when such individuals are off their guard they are left to themselves, as Jesus was. For this express purpose the Father withdrew His spirit from His Son, at the time he was to be crucified. Jesus had been with his Father, talked with Him, dwelt in His bosom, and knew all about heaven, about making the earth, about the transgression of man, and what would redeem the people, and that he was the character who was to redeem the sons of earth, and the earth itself from all sin that had come upon it. The light, knowledge, power, and glory with which he was clothed were far above, or exceeded that of all others who had been upon the earth after the fall, consequently at the very moment, at the hour when the crisis came for him to offer up his life, the Father withdrew Himself, withdrew His Spirit, and cast a vail over him. That is what made him sweat blood. If he had had the power of God upon him, he would not have sweat blood; but all was withdrawn from him, and a veil was cast over him, and he then plead with the Father not to forsake him. "No," says the Father, "You must have your trials, as well as others."
>
> So when individuals are blessed with visions, revelations, and great manifestations, look out, then the devil is nigh you, and you will be tempted in proportion to the vision, revelation, or manifestation you have received. Hence thousands, when they are off their guard, give way to the severe temptations which come upon them, and behold they are gone" (*Journal of Discourses* 3:205–6).

It doesn't sound like it will be smooth sailing between now and the Savior's return. Far too many people, including some Latter-day Saints, have joined forces with Satan and his armies (knowingly or ignorantly) in fighting God. They may not see it as such, but God's law of chastity has been scoffed at and disregarded by an increasing number of people inside and outside the Church. Marriage, as ordained by God between a man and a woman, has been legislated against in many countries, mixing up of genders is gaining strength and acceptance, abortion has been legalized, and the list goes endlessly on.

What an opportunity we have to be chosen to be on the Lord's team in these final seconds of the fourth quarter in the greatest battle of all time. We know who will win. The only question now is "which team will we be playing on?"

We need to expect that Satan will employ every weapon in his arsenal to try to destroy us. This book is written to give hope that we can win the battle against evil with the help of the Lord.

CHAPTER 4

Using Satan against Satan

Over the course of many years, I have been asked frequently about how to overcome undesirable behavior. Too many of those asking for help are trying, but they keep falling back into old habits. They ask if there isn't some strategy they could use that would help their efforts to overcome be more effective. I want to cite a few scriptures and see if the Lord has revealed some keys to help us be successful.

> Preach unto them repentance, and faith on the Lord Jesus Christ; teach them to humble themselves and to be meek and lowly in heart; **teach them to withstand every temptation of the devil, with their faith on the Lord Jesus Christ.** (Alma 37:33)

How do we use our faith in Christ to withstand EVERY temptation? He said in D&C 6:36: "Look unto me in every thought; doubt not, fear not."

How does that work? Use the undesirable thought as a catalyst—something to get you pointed in the right direction. For example, the second you recognize the temptation, you immediately use that as a reminder to look to the Savior. You might even say to yourself, "Thank you, Satan, for reminding me to—" and then have a list of activities that will lead you closer to the Savior. For example:

1. Say a prayer asking the Savior to strengthen and help you.

2. Read a chapter from the Book of Mormon or some other scripture.

3. Reread your patriarchal blessing.
4. Serve someone.
5. Call a spiritual friend or adult "just to chat."
6. Memorize a passage of scripture.
7. Listen to or read a recent conference talk.
8. Read an article from the *Ensign* or *New Era.*
9. Do some physical exercise or go for a jog.
10. The list can go on and on. List what takes **your** mind off the temptation and on to something that will help you become more Christlike.

Consider the parable the Savior gave in Matthew 12:43–45:

> When the unclean spirit is gone out of a man, he walketh through dry places, seeking rest, and findeth none.
>
> Then he saith, I will return into my house from whence I came out; and when he is come, he findeth *it* empty, swept, and garnished.
>
> Then goeth he, and taketh with himself seven other spirits more wicked than himself, and they enter in and dwell there: and the last *state* of that man is worse than the first.

Let me use an example from my younger days. When I was growing up, we had a soap that floated—Ivory Soap. One day while bathing, I decided to see how close I could get the floating soap to the rim of the bath tub without it going over. As I pushed the water back and forth, the soap moved higher with each wave.

Just as I was about to achieve my goal, my mother pounded on the door, wanting to know why all the water was gushing under the bathroom door and into the hallway.

My question: Why wouldn't the soap stay by the top of the tub on its own? You could see that the water level at the end of the tub was much higher than where I was sitting. In order for the water not to return, I would have had to do one of two things: (1) Quick freeze the water (not a good solution since I was sitting in the tub!) or (2) I must put something where I was sitting equal to the height of the soap. I also noticed that when the water (and soap) came back, it didn't stop where I was sitting but sloshed up higher behind me.

That is like the man who cleans out the devils (undesirable behavior) from his house but doesn't replace the previously occupied space with something desirable and of his choice. Then when he comes back, the house is empty, but rather than just invite one devil, he finds seven devils worse than the first. Can you see the connection? If you don't take the proactive approach and replace the undesirable habit with something of your choosing that is good, it will come back with a vengeance and be worse than it was before.

You may be struggling with pornography and/or self-abuse. You must realize that God instilled in your body those desires for physical intimacy. They are good because they are God-given. However, He put restrictions on how and when they are to be used (between husband and wife who are legally and lawfully married).

The devil always tries to pervert what God has given us and entice us to use it in a way that God has forbidden. Why not (as you detect Satan's effort to tempt you) say something like this: "Thank you, Satan, for reminding me what a wonderful power is in my body. You will never be anything other than the father of lies. Someday I will use that God-given power to copartner with God and my spouse in creating bodies for God's spirit children. For right now: Get thee behind me!"

If you consistently use Satan's temptations as a catalyst to remind you to do something that moves you toward becoming more Christlike, it won't be long before Satan will say, "Whoa! Not only is he not falling for my soul-destroying temptations, but he is also doing things that take him further away from my kingdom." Satan isn't intelligent—but he isn't stupid either. He will back off and hit you in a different area where he may have had success before. If you keep at it, the day will come when you will have blocked all of his temptations and find it relatively easy to overcome them.

Will you ever be completely free of temptations in this life? Probably not! But you can become completely successful in defending yourself against "all the fiery darts of the wicked" (see Ephesians 6:11–18, especially verse 16). I hope some of these ideas will help you. Know that the Savior is pulling for you. He said in D&C 64:2: "For verily I say unto you, I will that ye should overcome the world; wherefore I will have compassion upon you." And in D&C 50:35: "And by giving heed and doing these things which ye have received, and which ye shall hereafter receive—and the kingdom is given you of the Father, and **power to overcome all things** which are not ordained of him."

Note carefully the keys mentioned in D&C 50:35: By giving heed and doing the things written in the scriptures and by diligently following the counsel of living apostles and prophets, power will be given you to overcome all things that are not consistent with the commandments of God. The Lord did not put an asterisk saying that some things cannot be overcome. It doesn't matter what some professionals say about the impossibility of overcoming certain addictions. We have the word of God that everything falls under the divine umbrella of being overcome with the power of Christ.

CHAPTER 5

A Goliath That Keeps Getting Up

Likely we have all thrilled at the biblical story of David and Goliath (1 Samuel 17). It seems like the ultimate mismatch. Goliath is described as one whose height was "six cubits and a span," or, in our language, about nine feet and nine inches tall (see verse 4). The description of his armor and weapons leaves little to the imagination that he was more than the typical foe. David's courage in taking on such a giant creates multiple mental images.

I have thought many times how I would react if a giant of that size bellowed at me saying, "*Am* I a dog, that thou comest to me with staves? And the Philistine cursed David by his gods. And the Philistine said to David, Come to me, and I will give thy flesh unto the fowls of the air, and to the beasts of the field."

At that point, I can see myself retreating with haste and finding some hiding place. Not so with David. The scriptures record,

> Then said David to the Philistine, Thou comest to me with a sword, and with a spear, and with a shield: but I come to thee in the name of the LORD of hosts, the God of the armies of Israel, whom thou hast defied.
>
> This day will the LORD deliver thee into mine hand; and I will smite thee, and take thine head from thee; and I will give the carcases of the host of the Philistines this day unto the fowls of the air, and to the wild beasts of the earth; that all the earth may know that there is a God in Israel.

> And all this assembly shall know that the LORD saveth not with sword and spear: for the battle *is* the LORD's, and he will give you into our hands. (1 Samuel 17:43–47)

Then David ran toward the giant. The rest is history. Once Goliath was down, David took the giant's sword and cut off his head and held it up for everyone to see (verses 48–51).

That was the last time Israel had to deal with Goliath. However, each of us may have a "goliath" that we are battling. Whether it is a drug addiction, pornography, smoking, alcohol, a bad uncontrolled temper, or a hundred other things that we know we must overcome before being welcome in the presence of God.

Unlike David's goliath, we knock our goliath down, and before we know it, he is up again, challenging us, taunting us, and assuring us that we will never defeat him. What are we to do?

Envision Goliath lurking behind your closet door. You decide it's time to destroy him. You open the door and hit him as hard as you can on the nose. At first he laughs at you and knocks you down. Dejected, you think you are defeated, but following the counsel of living prophets, you determine to get back up and try again. That scenario is repeated several (maybe many) times. Then one day you hit your goliath and he falls backward and is down. Can you relax thinking you have won? If you do, you're in for a disappointing revelation. You open the closet door and there he is again.

However, having experienced some success, you hit him again and he goes down. Finally, over time, he doesn't get up again. Are you home free? Far from it! Now you look in the closet and see a couple smaller but still formidable goliaths standing there. However, encouraged by your success over the big goliath, you take them on. The result may be the same—you try, get knocked down, and get up and try again. Before long, you have conquered both of the smaller goliaths.

Now overcoming weakness has become somewhat of a game. You look and six much smaller goliaths have replaced the two smaller ones who replaced the large one. Systematically you dispatch these smaller goliaths one at a time.

Can you relax now that the majority of your weaknesses have been overcome? If you do you are in for a disappointment. If you let down your guard for one minute, each of the goliaths—including the big one, will raise its ugly head and try to blindside and destroy you. But with constant vigilance, you can keep all of the goliaths permanently destroyed.

What if one sneaks up and blindsides you and you slip back? He will loudly accuse you and say you never really won at all. That is why Satan is called "a liar from the beginning" (D&C 93:25). Can you be forgiven more than once for sinning? Satan would say "no," but (as expected) that is opposite from what the Lord said. "Yea, and as often as my people repent will I forgive them their trespasses against me" (Mosiah 26:30).

As cited before in a different content, John the Beloved saw our day and what Satan continues to do to discourage the Saints.

> And I heard a loud voice saying in heaven, Now is come salvation, and strength, and the kingdom of our God, and the power of his Christ: for **the accuser of our brethren** is cast down, which **accused them before our God day and night**.
>
> And they overcame him by the blood of the Lamb, and by the word of their testimony; and they loved not their lives unto the death.
>
> Therefore rejoice, *ye* heavens, and ye that dwell in them. Woe to the inhabiters of the earth and of the sea! for **the devil is come down unto you, having great wrath, because he knoweth that he hath but a short time.** (Revelation 12:10–12)

John gave two more keys to use in overcoming Satan: (1) We do it by the "blood of the Lamb"—accessing the Atonement of Christ; and (2) by "the word of our testimony"—using what we have learned and experienced in the past as reinforcements against Satan's never-ending attacks. Given what John saw, we can and should expect that Satan will intensify his efforts to destroy us using every tool in his nasty bag of tricks. Here is the Lord's admonition for our day: "Wherefore, gird up your loins and be prepared. Behold, the kingdom is yours, and the enemy shall not overcome" (D&C 38:9).

We may get knocked down a few times (or many times) by our goliaths, but the Lord's promise is that the enemy (although combined against us—see verse 12) will not overcome us. The Lord always keeps His promises.

CHAPTER 6

Satan's Tool of Addiction

The entire plan of salvation (on man's part) was built around man's ability to exercise agency to choose between good and evil. Lucifer, soon to become Satan, proposed a different plan. The Lord revealed to Moses:

> Wherefore, because that Satan rebelled against me, and **sought to destroy the agency of man, which I, the Lord God, had given him**, and also, that I should give unto him mine own power; by the power of mine Only Begotten, I caused that he should be cast down;
>
> And he became Satan, yea, even the devil, **the father of all lies, to deceive and to blind men, and to lead them captive at his will, even as many as would not hearken unto my voice.** (Moses 4:3–4)

What was his proposal that was rejected? It sounded pretty good that he was going to save every single soul, not losing a single one. Although cited before, this is an important key to identifying and overcoming Satan. Elder Bruce R. McConkie puts a different twist on Satan's plan—actually an expansion of what we normally think about when we consider what it means to destroy agency. He wrote,

> When the Eternal Father announced his plan of salvation—a plan that called for a mortal probation for all his spirit children; a plan that required a Redeemer to ransom men from the coming fall; **a plan that could only operate if mortal men had agency**—when the Father announced his plan, when he chose Christ as the Redeemer and rejected Lucifer, then there was war in heaven. That war was a war of words; it was a conflict of ideologies; it was a rebellion against God and his laws.

> Lucifer sought to dethrone God, to sit himself on the divine throne, and to save all men without reference to their works. **He sought to deny men their agency so they could not sin. He offered a mortal life of carnality and sensuality, of evil and crime and murder, following which all men would be saved.** His offer was a philosophical impossibility. There must needs be an opposition in all things. Unless there are opposites, there is nothing. There can be no light without darkness, no heat without cold, no virtue without vice, no good without evil, no salvation without damnation.
>
> And so, in the courts of heaven, the war of wars was waged. Christ and Michael and a mighty host of noble and great spirits preached the gospel of God and exhorted their brethren to follow the Father. Lucifer and his lieutenants preached another gospel, a gospel of fear and hate and lasciviousness and compulsion. They sought salvation without keeping the commandments, without overcoming the world, without choosing between opposites. (*The Millennial Messiah*, 666–67)

If you want to see Satan's plan in action, just look around the world. His war is being waged here and now with the exception that we don't usually physically see him and his followers. His game plan has never changed.

So compelling was Lucifer's argument that he persuaded one-third part of our Father's children to follow him. The Lord revealed to Joseph Smith:

> And it came to pass that Adam, being tempted of the devil—for, behold, the devil was before Adam, for he rebelled against me, saying, Give me thine honor, which is my power; and also **a third part of the hosts of heaven turned he away from me because of their agency**;
>
> And they were thrust down, and thus came the devil and his angels. (D&C 29:36–37)

Considering who Satan would have influence over, recall what the Lord revealed to Moses: "to **deceive** and to **blind** men, and to **lead them captive** at his will, even **as many as would not hearken unto my voice**" (Moses 4:4). So, the stage was set for unsuspecting mortals to fall prey to Satan's soul-destroying objectives.

Lehi taught,

> And I, Lehi, according to the things which I have read, must needs suppose that an angel of God, according to that which is written, had fallen from heaven; wherefore, he became a devil, having sought that which was evil before God.

> And because he had fallen from heaven, and had become miserable forever, he sought also the misery of all mankind. (2 Nephi 2:17–18)

So impressed was Lehi that he stated later in the same chapter:

> Wherefore, men are free according to the flesh; and all things are given them which are expedient unto man. And they are free to choose liberty and eternal life, through the great Mediator of all men, or to choose captivity and death, according to the captivity and power of the devil; for he seeketh that all men might be miserable like unto himself. (2 Nephi 2:27)

Paul understood well the war that would be waged as the spirit (which was determined to follow Christ in the pre-earth life) would war against the flesh, which from earliest days was carnal, sensual, and devilish (see Moses 5:13). He wrote,

> *This* I say then, Walk in the Spirit, and ye shall not fulfil the lust of the flesh.
>
> For the flesh lusteth against the Spirit, and the Spirit against the flesh: and these are contrary the one to the other: so that ye cannot do the things that ye would. (Galatians 5:16–17)

Since exercising our agency is the focal point of our mortal test, it seems only logical that Satan would attack us there. A wise Saint would carefully evaluate the possible pitfall of any and every activity, substance, habit, or pastime. Or, as the Lord revealed to Joseph Smith:

> But ye are commanded in all things to ask of God, who giveth liberally; and that which the Spirit testifies unto you even so I would that ye should do in all holiness of heart, walking uprightly before me, **considering the end of your salvation**, doing all things with prayer and thanksgiving, that ye may not be seduced by evil spirits, or doctrines of devils, or the commandments of men; for some are of men, and others of devils. (D&C 46:7)

It doesn't require a PhD in theology to see how becoming addicted to drugs or alcohol destroys the individual and places extreme hardships on those who know and love him. Satan isn't intelligent, but he isn't stupid either. He realizes that if he hits you cold with some addictive substance or activity, he will likely fail to seduce you. So, like Amalickiah in the Book of Mormon, he poisons us by degrees. This is how Mormon recorded it:

"And it came to pass that Amalickiah caused that one of his servants should administer poison by degrees to Lehonti, that he died" (Alma 47:18). Nephi echoes the same warning: "He [Satan] leadeth them by the neck with a flaxen cord [one that is easily broken], until he bindeth them with his strong cords forever" (2 Nephi 26:22).

It generally isn't the first drink, the first exposure to pornography, or the first experimentation with drugs that addicts a person (although some drugs are addictive or lethal with the first experience). But by degrees a person loses his agency until, like Nephi said, "And others will he [the devil] pacify, and lull them away into carnal security, that they will say: All is well in Zion; yea, Zion prospereth, all is well—and thus the devil cheateth their souls, and **leadeth them away carefully down to hell**" (2 Nephi 28:21).

It seems there isn't any practice, substance, or activity that, in and of itself, is innocent that the devil hasn't turned into one of his tools to destroy the agency of man. But the initial choice to turn toward Satan and away from God has to be made by each individual as they exercise their agency.

Joseph Smith taught,

> He [Joseph Smith] commenced his observations by remarking that the kindness of our Heavenly Father called for our heartfelt gratitude. He then observed that Satan was generally blamed for the evils which we did, but if he was the cause of all our wickedness, men could not be condemned. The **devil could not compel mankind to do evil**; **all was voluntary**. Those who resisted the Spirit of God, would be liable to be led into temptation, and then the association of heaven would be withdrawn from those who refused to be made partakers of such great glory. God would not exert any compulsory means, and the devil could not; and such ideas as were entertained [on these subjects] by many were absurd. (*Teachings of the Prophet Joseph Smith,* 187)

The purpose for citing this passage again is what Joseph Smith indicated as the beginning point of our downfall or addiction: "Those who resisted the Spirit of God . . ." If we will pay attention, the Spirit will warn and forewarn when we are heading into dangerous territory. Failure to heed those warnings puts the burden of consequences squarely on our shoulders.

Is there hope for one who has made foolish choices? Yes! Limhi, a Nephite king who had learned by sad experience the painful consequences of turning their collective backs on God, said,

> But if ye will turn to the Lord with full purpose of heart, and put your trust in him, and serve him with all diligence of mind, if ye do this,

> he will, according to his own will and pleasure, deliver you out of bondage. (Mosiah 7:33)

The answer on where to start overcoming any addiction or undesirable practice or habit is to turn to the Savior and plead for His help. The Lord said, "That your enemies may not have power over you; that you may be preserved in all things; that you may be enabled to keep my laws; that every bond may be broken wherewith the enemy seeketh to destroy my people" (D&C 44:5).

The next logical, easy-to-do step you can take to free yourself from undesirable addictions is outlined by Isaiah: "*Is* not this the **fast** that I have chosen? to loose the bands of wickedness, to undo the heavy burdens, and to let the oppressed go free, and that ye break every yoke?" (Isaiah 58:6). The specific purpose for fasting is to "loose the bands of wickedness"—indicating that you are encircled by those bands. "To undo the heavy burdens"—denoting that you are carrying unnecessary burdens. "To let the oppressed go free"—suggesting you are weighed down or trampled down with some substance or habit. "To break every yoke"—note Isaiah did not put an asterisk by "every." With the help of the Lord, you can break **every** yoke.

Are there some afflictions of the mind brought on by drug or alcohol abuse that cannot be reversed? In outlining the purpose of the Savior coming and the experiences He went through so He could have a firsthand knowledge of what plagued every person on earth, Alma taught,

> And he shall go forth, **suffering pains and afflictions and temptations of every kind**; and this that the word might be fulfilled which saith he will take upon him the pains and the sicknesses of his people.
>
> And he will take upon him death, that he may loose the bands of death which bind his people; and **he will take upon him their infirmities**, that his bowels may be filled with mercy, according to the flesh, that he may know according to the flesh how to succor his people according to their infirmities. (Alma 7:11–12)

He didn't say the Savior would reverse the infirmity (which He can if and when He chooses) but that He knows how to do what is best for them here in mortality and in eternity. Trust that He will do what is best for you in the eternal scheme of things.

Perhaps an honest analysis of what you do, how much time it consumes, does it limit your ability to move forward with things you really want in life, and so on, would be a good starting place to devise your plan to move forward. Only you can answer these questions. Perhaps doing all things "considering the end of your salvation" is more important than we sometimes give it credit. When you stand knowing that it is the last day of your mortal experience, are you able to look back without regret, without saying, "I wish I would have," or, "I wish I wouldn't have"?

Postponing taking control of your life may not be easy, depending on how long and how deeply you have allowed the enemy of your soul to lead you toward hell, but one thing is for sure—the longer you put it off, the more difficult it will be and the less time you'll have to prepare to meet God.

To say you'll just put off taking control of your life until the next life is naively dangerous. Amulek taught and warned,

> For behold, this life is the time for men to prepare to meet God; yea, behold the day of this life is the day for men to perform their labors.
>
> And now, as I said unto you before, as ye have had so many witnesses, therefore, I beseech of you that ye do not procrastinate the day of your repentance until the end; for after this day of life, which is given us to prepare for eternity, behold, if we do not improve our time while in this life, then cometh the night of darkness wherein there can be no labor performed.
>
> Ye cannot say, when ye are brought to that awful crisis, that I will repent, that I will return to my God. Nay, ye cannot say this; for that same spirit which doth possess your bodies at the time that ye go out of this life, that same spirit will have power to possess your body in that eternal world.
>
> For behold, if ye have procrastinated the day of your repentance even until death, behold, ye have become subjected to the spirit of the devil, and he doth seal you his; therefore, the Spirit of the Lord hath withdrawn from you, and hath no place in you, and the devil hath all power over you; and this is the final state of the wicked. (Alma 34:32–35)

It is interesting to note that "that same spirit" that Amulek said would possess your body when you leave mortality may be referring to the Spirit of the Lord or the spirit of the devil. Surely your spirit will be alive and well in the spirit world, but whose spirit will have influence over you? Now really is the time to bring yourself under the influence of the Lord's Spirit so there will be no question about who will possess your body in the eternal worlds.

CHAPTER 7

Using the Whole Armor of God

If the Lord had not given us the weapons to fight the adversary, it would seem grossly unfair. However, He revealed to Paul and again to Joseph Smith what is necessary to successfully win the war with Satan and his followers. Paul wrote,

> Put on the whole armour of God, that ye may be able to stand against the wiles of the devil.
>
> For we wrestle not against flesh and blood, but against principalities, against powers, against the rulers of the darkness of this world, against spiritual wickedness in high *places.*
>
> Wherefore take unto you the whole armour of God, that ye may be able to withstand in the evil day, and having done all, to stand.
>
> Stand therefore, having your loins girt about with truth, and having on the breastplate of righteousness;
>
> And your feet shod with the preparation of the gospel of peace;
>
> Above all, taking the shield of faith, wherewith ye shall be able to quench all the fiery darts of the wicked.
>
> And take the helmet of salvation, and the sword of the Spirit, which is the word of God:
>
> Praying always with all prayer and supplication in the Spirit, and watching thereunto with all perseverance and supplication for all saints. (Ephesians 6:11–18)

It is instructive to note what parts of the armor are used to protect us against "the wiles of the devil." Paul begins with the "loins"—our reproductive capabilities. Why start there? Joseph F. Smith gave this prophetic insight in March 1914:

> There are at least three dangers that threaten the Church within, and the authorities need to awaken to the fact that the people should be warned unceasingly against them. As I see these, they are flattery of prominent men in the world, false educational ideas, and sexual impurity.
>
> But the third subject mentioned—personal purity, is perhaps of greater importance than either of the other two. We believe in one standard of morality for men and women. If purity of life is neglected, all other dangers set in upon us like the rivers of waters when the flood gates are opened. (*Gospel Doctrine: Selections from the Sermons and Writings of Joseph F. Smith* [Salt Lake City: Deseret Book, 1971], 312–13)

There is no question in today's world that the law of chastity is widely disregarded, and yet Alma calls it "the sin next to murder" (see Alma 39:5–6). Indeed, Isaiah called it right when he said, "Woe unto them that call evil good, and good evil; that put darkness for light, and light for darkness; that put bitter for sweet, and sweet for bitter!" (Isaiah 5:20). However, truth never changes. It is the same yesterday, today, and forever (see D&C 93:24). People can break themselves against the Ten Commandments, judges and legislators can make laws legalizing sin, but that doesn't impact or change the commandments of God.

The next part of the armor Paul described is the "breastplate of righteousness." President Harold B. Lee talked about the whole armor of God and said the breastplate covers the vital organs, especially the heart. What protects us? Righteousness. If we would do as Alma instructed his son Helaman to "look to God and live" (see Alma 37:47), we could avoid most of the suffering and heartache that attends the consequences of breaking God's commandments. It is simple if we adopt the adage, "What God says is right is right. And what God says is wrong is wrong!" We need to quit trying to counsel God as to right and wrong. In fact, God commanded, "Seek not to counsel your God" (D&C 22:4).

The third article of armor is the feet. They are shod with the "gospel of peace." Consider what feet do for us: they take us toward our goals. If our goal is to go where the Prince of Peace (Christ) is, then this part of the armor makes many of our decisions very easy. Since Christ is in the highest degree of the celestial kingdom, anything or any activity that would act as a detour taking us away from our goal should be avoided. Since the Lord has outlined the criteria for entering into His House (the temple), and since He would not have a different set of standards for entering into His eternal presence (being an Unchangeable God—see Mosiah 2:22), we need to compare our activities to the questions asked when we renew our temple recommend. If we can honestly answer those fifteen questions, we have our feet shod with the gospel that will eventually lead us to the celestial kingdom.

Next consider the "helmet of salvation." The helmet covers our head or our intellect. In today's pseudo-intellectual world, which Paul describes as "Ever learning, and never able to come to the knowledge of the truth" (2 Timothy 3:7), any and every theory is used to eliminate God as an intelligent power in creating the world and everything in it. If Satan can ever get a Latter-day Saint to question the great plan of salvation, forget that he or she is a child of God, destroy our faith in the eternal nature of the rewards that attend faithfully living the commandments, and scoff at the power of the Atonement of Christ, then, like dominos, every other commandment will fall. It is our faith in the plan of salvation that gives us the courage to withstand the attacks of Satan by our faith in Christ. Alma taught, "Preach unto them repentance, and faith on the Lord Jesus Christ; teach them to humble themselves and to be meek and lowly in heart; **teach them to withstand every temptation of the devil, with their faith on the Lord Jesus Christ**" (Alma 37:33).

Next is the "shield of faith, wherewith ye shall be able to quench all the fiery darts of the wicked." Where does a soldier in a hand-to-hand battle use a shield? Wherever he is being attacked! If you are being battered intellectually, put the shield of faith over your head until your intellectual abilities are sufficiently strong to withstand the satanic attacks. If you are being tempted to abuse the powers of procreation, put the shield over your loins knowing full well that eventually you will thank God that you didn't give in to the lusts of the flesh and have to look back with regret that you surrendered that which is most precious to the lusts of the moment. If you are tempted to break the Word of Wisdom or embrace the ever-shifting philosophies of men (for example gay marriage, transgender privileges, and so forth) put the shield over your heart. If you are tempted to take a detour that could possibly disqualify you from going to the temple, put the shield over your feet.

Finally, even if you had all of these defensive parts of the armor firmly in place, you would still eventually lose the battle because you have no offensive weapon. The offensive weapon is "the Spirit." With it, you cannot fail. Without it, you cannot succeed. The Spirit quickens your mind and strengthens you in all areas. Without the Spirit, you are facing an adversary with over 6000 years' experience and with resources that far exceed your natural strength.

There is, however, one part of the anatomy that is not covered by the armor of God—the back. We cannot run away from the battle with Satan. We must meet him head on knowing that with the help of Christ, we can defeat him. Helaman, in warning and teaching his sons, said,

> And now, my sons, remember, remember that it is upon the rock of our Redeemer, who is Christ, the Son of God, that ye must build your foundation; that **when** the devil shall send forth his mighty winds, yea, his shafts in the whirlwind, yea, **when** all his hail and his mighty storm shall beat upon you, it shall have no power over you to drag you down to the gulf of misery and endless wo, because of the rock upon which ye are built, which is a sure foundation, a foundation whereon if men build they cannot fall. (Helaman 5:12)

Note that he did not say "if" the devil should attack but "when."

Almost as an after-thought, Paul encourages us to "pray always with all prayer and supplication in the Spirit." The Lord adds a punctuation mark when he warned us in these latter days to "pray always, that you may come off conqueror; yea, that you may conquer Satan, and that you may escape the hands of the servants of Satan that do uphold his work" (D&C 10:5).

If we take seriously the "whole armor of God," we not only protect ourselves but also have the ability to arm those around us. The sooner we consciously arm ourselves, the sooner we gain control over the destroyer of souls.

CHAPTER 8

Don't Identify Yourself as the "Old Man of Sin"

One of the wonderful, but not well understood, doctrines of the gospel is what effect the Atonement of Christ has on us when we repent. Paul stated the obvious: "For all have sinned, and come short of the glory of God" (Romans 3:23). We know from scriptures and continued urging from living prophets and apostles that we all need to repent.

How can we tell if our efforts at repentance are complete and acceptable? Many formulas have been suggested, but the Lord's formula is the simplest and most complete. He said,

> Behold, he who has repented of his sins, the same is forgiven, and I, the Lord, remember them no more. By this ye may know if a man repenteth of his sins—behold, he will **confess** them and **forsake** them. (D&C 58:42–43)

That seems pretty simple and straightforward—confess and forsake. The "confess" part entails voluntarily, without being coerced or found out, admitting or owning that we have sinned. Sin is the "willful transgression of the law."

"Now they did not sin ignorantly, for they knew the will of God concerning them, for it had been taught unto them; therefore they did wilfully rebel against God" (3 Nephi 6:18). Violating the law of God without knowing the commandment falls into a different category than willful rebellion.

Once a repentant person "owns" his sin by confessing to the Lord, the offended one (if reasonable), and to God's representative (the bishop or stake president if the sin is of a nature that would put membership in the Church or the privilege of temple attendance in jeopardy), then that is all that is required. Once a person has confessed completely, there is no need to re-confess again and again. That is one of the tactics that Satan uses to stop us from progressing. It is called "confessionitus." Satan, the liar from the beginning" (D&C 93:25), will whisper over and over again, "What about this little thing you left out of your confession?" Or, "You forgot to include that detail." At the end of your confession to the bishop, pause and silently pray to know if there are additional details you need to disclose. If nothing comes to mind, consider the matter closed and don't return to it.

Forsaking one's sins means to resolve not to do it again. Is there a possibility that, in spite of your resolve, you will slip and fall? Yes, but unless you calculatingly and knowingly sin, your former sins will not return.

Some have struggled with the Lord's declaration in D&C 82:7 that states, "And now, verily I say unto you, I, the Lord, will not lay any sin to your charge; go your ways and sin no more; but unto that soul who sinneth shall the former sins return, saith the Lord your God."

Envision in your mind facing the sun (Son). All of your shadowy past sins are behind you as you bask in the welcoming rays that radiate from Him. You slip and fall but you are still trying. You are still facing the sun (Son). Your past sins do not return. It isn't until you "willfully" turn your back on the Son that His light now illuminates past sins and they return.

Now the Lord says you are forgiven and He remembers them no more. Will you still remember them? Yes. Why? Possibly one reason is so that we don't sin again. Will there ever come a time in mortality when you will "remember them no more?" Yes, in the Lord's due time, the memory of past transgressions will be erased. In some cases that seems to happen fairly soon, and in other cases, years pass before the memory fades into oblivion.

What has happened to you? According to Paul, you have "crucified the old man of sin."

> Know ye not, that so many of us as were baptized into Jesus Christ were baptized into his death?
>
> Therefore we are buried with him by baptism into death: that like as Christ was raised up from the dead by the glory of the Father, even so we also should walk in newness of life.
>
> For if we have been planted together in the likeness of his death, we shall be also *in the likeness* of *his* resurrection:

> Knowing this, that **our old man is crucified with *him***, that the body of sin might be destroyed, that henceforth we should not serve sin. (Romans 6:3–6)

Alma the Younger, after an angelic visit and suffering repentance nigh unto death, added this important insight:

> For, said he, I have repented of my sins, and have been redeemed of the Lord; behold I am born of the Spirit.
>
> And the Lord said unto me: Marvel not that all mankind, yea, men and women, all nations, kindreds, tongues and people, must be born again; yea, born of God, changed from their carnal and fallen state, to a state of righteousness, being redeemed of God, becoming his sons and daughters;
>
> And thus they become **new creatures**; and unless they do this, they can in nowise inherit the kingdom of God. (Mosiah 27:24–26)

Once you have "crucified the old man of sin" and have been "born again and become a new creature in Christ," the Atonement of Christ has worked its magic. Satan will tell you many times that you are still the "old man of sin." Unfortunately, too many of my former students and others continue to identify with the old man of sin.

When I was growing up, we had a Sunday School teacher who taught his version of repentance. He brought a piece of board and placed it on the table. Then he took several nails and pounded them into the board, saying with each nail, "This is sin." Then he took a claw hammer and extracted each nail, saying, "This is repentance." It was impressive to my young mind but incorrect. Notably, the nail holes were still in the board. Even if we put putty and shellac to cover the holes, is that a fair representation of what repentance does? With the use of an electron microscope, each davit would still be visible. The Atonement throws away the old board and gives you a brand new one.

The key is to recognize who you are "**now**." Are you the new creature, or are you the old man of sin? If you must still identify yourself as the old man of sin, when do you get to stop? When you go to the temple? When you get married? When you are 65? When you die? When you are resurrected? If the Atonement of Christ doesn't make us a new creature, it hasn't done what the Lord said it would do. You need to honestly ask yourself, when confronted with past sins, "Has the new creature ever done that?" You are no longer the "old man of sin," so let the Atonement make you a new creature.

Then, if you need to confess past sins, where do you stop? Must you tell about when you when you smoked a cigarette when you were sixteen? Stole a candy bar when you were twelve? When you said a swear word when you were ten? Can't you see that if the Atonement doesn't make you a new creature, there is no logical stopping point in your confession, and you really aren't any closer to being a celestial kingdom candidate than before you repented.

Perhaps this is where the rubber meets the road in the gospel. When queried about past sins, can you truthfully say (as the new creature in Christ) that you never did them? True, the old man of sin (who was crucified by the Atonement of Christ) had sinned, but you are no longer him. Enjoy the newness of life. A clean, fresh start every time you truly repent.

CHAPTER 9

Avoid Using Your Sinful Past to Teach

In the last chapter, we discussed how to repent and become a new creature in Christ. Now we need to identify and caution against another of Satan's clever tricks: using your sinful past to help others avoid making the same mistake.

You might say, "What about Alma the Younger? He used his past to instruct and warn his sons." While that is true, Alma's experience was such an open and well-known event that everyone knew about it. You are no Alma the Younger. You also might learn from the example of modern prophets and apostles. How many times have you heard them confess past sins?

Why not use your sinful past to teach? There are two obvious potential downfalls. First, if you have gained enough prominence to be asked to speak or teach, you likely have (like it or not) become somewhat of a hero figure or role model in the eyes of your audience. If you relate a past sin or transgression to them, you run the risk of them seeing what you are now and thinking, *Well, if he can sin and still turn out that good, why couldn't I do the same?*

It may be true that they can sin and still turn out all right with sincere repentance, but many may take that first calculated step off the covenant path and lose their way in the mists of darkness that obscure their vision of the tree of life (see 1 Nephi 8).

President George Albert Smith said it best:

> There is a line of demarcation well defined between the Lord's territory and the devil's territory. If you will stay on the Lord's side of the line you will be under his influence and will have no desire to do wrong; but if you cross to the devil's side of that line one inch you are in the tempter's power and if he is successful, you will not be able to think or even reason properly because you will have lost the Spirit of the Lord (in Conference Report, Oct. 1945).

Far too many people, young and old, have decided to sample the alluring drink offered by those in the large and spacious building, only to find that the first taste was addictive and eventually spiritually lethal.

The other thing often not viewed or talked about is the pain and sorrow you went through before you received a remission of your sins. Alma the Younger described his experience this way:

> I say unto you, unless this be the case, they must be cast off; and this I know, because I was like to be cast off.
>
> Nevertheless, after wading through much tribulation, **repenting nigh unto death**, the Lord in mercy hath seen fit to snatch me out of an everlasting burning, and I am born of God.
>
> My soul hath been redeemed from the gall of bitterness and bonds of iniquity. **I was in the darkest abyss**; but now I behold the marvelous light of God. **My soul was racked with eternal torment**; but I am snatched, and my soul is pained no more. (Mosiah 27:27–29)

Later, to his son, he recounted,

> But I was racked with eternal torment, for my soul was harrowed up to the greatest degree and racked with all my sins.
>
> Yea, I did remember all my sins and iniquities, for which I was tormented with the pains of hell; yea, I saw that I had rebelled against my God, and that I had not kept his holy commandments. . . . And now, for three days and for three nights was I racked, even with the pains of a damned soul.
>
> And it came to pass that as I was thus racked with torment, while I was harrowed up by the memory of my many sins. (Alma 36:12–13, 16–17)

Alma then described turning to Christ.

Without your audience seeing the whole picture of your past and your struggles to return, they are only seeing the sweetness of the Savior's forgiving power. Why run the risk?

The second risk you take in using your past to teach is the chance that your audience will dismiss you as a hypocrite. "Why should we listen to you? You teach one thing and live another!" While their judgment is unfair, you have brought it upon yourself.

How do you use the lessons you have learned in the school of hard knocks without falling prey to either of the above possibilities? It really is easy. Rather than referring to your past sins in the first person, why not label them for what they are—mistakes and sins made by the "old man of sin"? You have repented and the Atonement of Christ has made you a new creature. The new creature has never sinned in the manner the old man of sin has, so why not say, "I have a close friend (without naming yourself as the old man of sin), who did thus." You can describe in vivid detail the struggle and pain he had in getting back on the covenant path. Now your audience can still look at you, admire the person you are, and say, "I'm sure glad I'm not the 'old man of sin' he is describing. I want to do all in my power to avoid the mistakes the speaker is talking about."

If you say, "Well, when I was the 'old man of sin,' I did some dumb things," the audience may not be able to distinguish between you now and your former self. It just isn't worth the risk. The other inescapable risk is that you are re-identifying yourself as the "old man of sin." Satan will take advantage of that, and at the most inappropriate time, when you are at your greatest vulnerability, he will throw it in your face. He'll say, "By your own admission, you are still the old man of sin!" Don't give him the bullets he needs to destroy you and those you teach.

CHAPTER 10

Satan's Use of the Memory of Past Sins

One of Satan's most effective tactics is to bring back, usually at the most inopportune time, your past mistakes or sins. It may not be possible to completely stop him from employing this method of destruction, but you can turn the tables on him and use it to move you toward greater spirituality.

Being aware of his destructive efforts puts you on notice when to redouble your guard against him. For example, you may meet a person you were inappropriately intimate with many years ago. Satan will try to get you to re-create the feelings and memories long since repented of. In rare cases, the person you were intimate with may not have changed their lifestyle and may actively try to entice you to commit sexual sins with them again. Be especially cautious if your marriage is experiencing normal challenges and you are tempted to believe that "the grass is greener on the other side of the fence."

With the common portrayal of immorality on the internet and in movies, it is doubly likely that Satan will try to capitalize on the seeds of immorality he has planted in your mind through the numerous entertainment media you may have been exposed to.

Be vigilant so that when you return to a place you engaged in inappropriate behavior, and Satan does all in his power to recreate the emotions you felt many years before, you will be able to withstand his enticements. The classic example is the reformed alcoholic returning to the bar where he "enjoyed" many hours of socialization with his drinking buddies. Satan may lure you into such an environment just to see if any of your friends are still there—

assuring you that you are not going to drink but only observe. Far too many repenting Saints have fallen prey to such a ploy and looked back with regret that they were not more cautious.

Even smells and tastes can bring back memories of sins you may have committed. When I was very young, my grandfather's brother visited at the cabin where my brother and I were staying with our grandparents. Uncle Ren smoked a pipe with cherry tobacco. The smell was unusual and pleasant to my brother and me. Neither of us smoked. Many years later, I was walking down a street in New York City. A man walking in the opposite direction was smoking a pipe with the same cherry tobacco Uncle Ren had smoked. Immediately, I was transported in my mind to the cabin with all the pleasant memories associated with that time many years previously. I still don't smoke (not even tempted to), but I am confident that whenever I come into the presence of a person smoking cherry tobacco, I'll have that memory (from seventy-plus years ago) renewed.

For many years, I thought films were produced just to entertain people. At first, they seemed so innocent and fun. Then, over the years, it became obvious that the devil had his fingers in the content of the movies. All the way from "damn" in *Gone with the Wind* to today's language that offends anyone who has not been lullabied by the entertainment industry's progressive decline. Nothing is off limits. Even the news, comedy shows, and interviews with high governmental officials or other celebrities include language that was shocking and unacceptable just a few years ago.

From couples sleeping in separate beds in former days, to today's sex scenes leaving nothing to the imagination, the seeds of immorality are being sown endlessly to an audience either unsuspecting of its influence or willingly accepting its content.

Pornography has a like impact. A person might not have experienced the sin, but viewing it repeatedly desensitizes his conscience and puts him at greater risk of surrendering to it in the future. If it wasn't so serious, it would be humorous how modern society feeds the ugly monster of pornography with its most degrading perversions and then wrings its collective hands when someone acts out what they have been watching.

How can one live in the world but not be of the world? It may not be possible to completely avoid all of the evil influences around us, but we may be able to control them to a large degree. The most obvious way to lessen the grasp that past experiences, places, and entertainment have on us is to avoid, where possible, those persons, places, and environments. You don't have to associate with people you were previously inappropriate with. You don't have to frequent places where you engaged in sinful practices. You can avoid entertainment that plants seeds that eventually could lead you to sin. You can refrain from accessing internet sites or videos that drive the Spirit from you.

Although used before in previous chapters, the key is found in ten words the Savior spoke: "Look unto me in every thought; doubt not, fear not!" (D&C 6:36). When a person begins to take control of his thoughts, then the Spirit can warn and forewarn when he is heading down a path that will take him away from the pathway to exaltation.

Instead of taking the easy route of tuning in to entertainment produced by a rapidly deteriorating telestial world, take the more challenging, growth-producing avenue to fill your leisure hours with something that has eternal significance. Perhaps writing your personal history, doing some family search, more frequently attending the temple, visiting relatives or friends, perhaps (if you are really brave) writing a book sharing your experience and wisdom with a broader circle.

Take some time to ponder and see if the Lord will reveal how He would have you use your leisure hours. From personal experience, I would suspect that whatever inspiration comes to you will take you outside your comfort zone. With each activity you engage in that is inspired from the other side, you will find that controlling the unwanted and undesirable flashbacks Satan bombards you with will become progressively easier.

The more you ponder and reflect upon past experience **while under the influence of the Spirit**, the more principles of righteousness you will see to enrich your life. Joseph Smith and Oliver Cowdery said this after their baptism and receiving the Holy Ghost:

> Our minds being now enlightened, we began to have the scriptures laid open to our understandings, and the true meaning and intention of their more mysterious passages revealed unto us in a manner which we never could attain to previously, nor ever before had thought of. (Joseph Smith—History 1:74)

You may not be dealing with scriptures, but experience will show that when the Spirit is upon you, you will see things in your past experiences that you have never recognized before. One thing that many people have confided in me during counseling sessions is how protected they were during times when they could have been killed, injured, or committed serious sins, but for some unknown reason, they were spared. I presume that many of you, upon serious reflections, will say the same thing. That is where you begin to see that the hand of the Lord has been over you even when you were unaware of it.

Using the Spirit to illuminate your past and help you learn from past mistakes is one of the most enlightening experiences you can possibly have. Then, not using specifics of past transgression (previously discussed in detail in this chapter), you can help others who are heading down the same path you have repented of and are now moving forward.

Someday you will look back at everything that has happened in your life and thank the Lord for the learning opportunities. Are you better off for having sinned than if you hadn't? No, but the Lord can use you to help others avoid Satan's deceptive tactics.

In a final plea after witnessing the entire destruction of his people, Moroni penned something that we may adopt for our purpose in writing to a broader audience than just our immediate family.

> Condemn me not because of mine imperfection, neither my father, because of his imperfection, neither them who have written before him; but rather give thanks unto God that he hath made manifest unto you our imperfections, **that ye may learn to be more wise than we have been.** (Mormon 9:31)

Remembering past mistakes can be depressing, or it can be exhilarating. Only you can determine which impact you will allow those recurring memories to have. In a much smaller way but equally as important, what has been written in this book about the experiences of others and their attempts to win the battle with evil parallels what Moroni said about the Book of Mormon. You can become part of the conversation of the ages where we use what has happened in our lives to enrich the lives of those who follow.

CHAPTER 11

INFLUENCED VS. POSSESSED

George Q. Cannon, who served as a counselor to four Presidents of the Church, said on November 13, 1864:

> There are influences in the atmosphere that are invisible to us that, while we are here upon the earth, we ought to resist with all our might, mind, and strength—influences which, if we would be led by them, would lead us to destruction—influences that are opposed to the Spirit of God—influences that would bring upon us destruction here and hereafter, if we would yield to them. These influences we have to resist. We have to resist the spirit of adultery, the spirit of whoredom, the spirit of drunkenness, the spirit of theft, and every other evil influence and spirit, that we may continually overcome; and, when we have finished our work on the earth, be prepared to govern and control those influences, and exercise power over them, in the presence of our Father and God. I have no doubt that many of my brethren and sisters have sensibly felt in various places and at various times evil influences around them. Brother Joseph Smith gave an explanation of this. There are places in the Mississippi Valley where the influence or the presence of invisible spirits are very perceptibly felt. He said that numbers had been slain there in war, and that there were evil influences or spirits which affect the spirits of those who have tabernacles on the earth. I myself have felt those influences in other places besides the continent of America; I have felt them on the old battlegrounds on the Sandwich Islands. I have come to the conclusion that if our eyes were open to see the spirit world around us, we should feel differently on this subject than we do; we would not be so unguarded and careless, and so indifferent whether we had the spirit and power of God with us or not; but we would be continually watchful and prayerful to

> our heavenly Father for His Holy Spirit and His holy angels to be around about us to strengthen us to overcome every evil influence" (*Journal of Discourses*, 11:29–30).

With that insight from President Cannon, we might easily make the connection that when we are having a bad day, it may not just be a bad day but one where evil spirits are trying to influence us to deviate from the covenant path.

From the very earliest times, Satan has been trying to dissuade mortals from following God's pathway to happiness. Beginning with the children of Adam and Eve, Satan presented his counter-gospel after Adam and Eve had held a family home evening explaining the plan of salvation. Moses records,

> And Adam and Eve blessed the name of God, and they made all things known unto their sons and their daughters.
>
> And Satan came among them, saying: I am also a son of God; and he commanded them, saying: Believe it not; and they believed it not, and they loved Satan more than God. And men began from that time forth to be carnal, sensual, and devilish. (Moses 5:12–13)

Saul, the first king of Israel, had "bad days" that his servants readily recognized. Note how the writer of 1 Samuel described it:

> But the Spirit of the LORD departed from Saul, and an evil spirit which was not from the LORD troubled him.
>
> And Saul's servants said unto him, Behold now, an evil spirit which is not of God troubleth thee. (Joseph Smith Translation, 1 Samuel 16:14–15)
>
> And it came to pass, when the *evil* spirit which was not from God was upon Saul, that David took an harp, and played with his hand: so Saul was refreshed, and was well, and the evil spirit departed from him. (Joseph Smith Translation, 1 Samuel 16:23)

It is interesting that 2900 years after Adam and Eve became mortals, people still readily acknowledged the devil and evil spirits as the cause of mental problems. It is also noteworthy that good music was the remedy that Saul used to rid himself of that depressing influence.

Seldom, if ever, in today's "enlightened" world do people or professionals ascribe some of our mental challenges to the influences of evil spirits.

An angel awakened King Benjamin to give him a message he was to deliver the next day to his people. The angel said,

> For behold, the time cometh, and is not far distant, that with power, the Lord Omnipotent who reigneth, who was, and is from all eternity to all eternity, shall come down from heaven among the children of men, and shall dwell in a tabernacle of clay, and shall go forth amongst men, working mighty miracles, such as healing the sick, raising the dead, causing the lame to walk, the blind to receive their sight, and the deaf to hear, and curing all manner of diseases.
>
> **And he shall cast out devils, or the evil spirits which dwell in the hearts of the children of men.** (Mosiah 3:5–6)

While it is apparent that evil spirits can and do influence people's moods and actions, it also seems true that, with conscious effort, they can resist those feelings. One of the most effective ways of ridding one's self from evil influences is to seek out places and people who radiate the light of the Spirit. Light and darkness cannot dwell together. If you are trying to help others who are struggling, get them to an environment where you know the Spirit of the Lord is. Either the Spirit of the Lord will withdraw or the spirit of the devil. Like King Saul, good music can help drive that negative, dark feeling away. A visit to the temple grounds (or entering the temple if they have a recommend) counteracts those evil influences. The list can be expanded using examples others have used to bounce back from a "bad day."

Being possessed by evil spirits or devils is considerably more serious than having just the influence of evil spirits. As cited above, one of the things Christ did during His mortal ministry was to "cast out devils or the evil spirits which dwell in the hearts of the children of men" (Mosiah 3:6).

When a person is possessed of the devil, he is no longer in control of his actions. The story of the Gadarene man who was possessed demonstrates some vital information. Here is the account:

> And when he [Christ] went forth to land, there met him out of the city a certain man, which had devils long time, and ware no clothes, neither abode in *any* house, but in the tombs.
>
> When he saw Jesus, he cried out, and fell down before him, and with a loud voice said, What have I to do with thee, Jesus, *thou* Son of God most high? I beseech thee, torment me not.
>
> (For he had commanded the unclean spirit to come out of the man. For oftentimes it had caught him: and he was kept bound with chains

> and in fetters; and he brake the bands, and was driven of the devil into the wilderness.)
>
> And Jesus asked him, saying, What is thy name? And he said, Legion: because many devils were entered into him.
>
> And they besought him that he would not command them to go out into the deep.
>
> And there was there an herd of many swine feeding on the mountain: and they besought him that he would suffer them to enter into them. And he suffered them.
>
> Then went the devils out of the man, and entered into the swine: and the herd ran violently down a steep place into the lake, and were choked.
>
> When they that fed *them* saw what was done, they fled, and went and told *it* in the city and in the country.
>
> Then they went out to see what was done; and came to Jesus, and found the man, out of whom the devils were departed, sitting at the feet of Jesus, clothed, and in his right mind: and they were afraid.
>
> They also which saw *it* told them by what means he that was possessed of the devils was healed. (Luke 8:27–36)

It is noteworthy that while possessed of evil spirits, the man's physical strength was greatly increased. In Mark's account (see Mark 5:1–19), the man cut himself with stones and cried day and night. No one could "tame" him, another fact that helps define the abilities of an evil spirit. When Christ demanded of the evil spirit what his name was, indicating that they, like us, have individual names, the evil spirit said they were "Legion: because many devils were entered into him." It is obvious that more than one evil spirit can possess a single human body at the same time. We do not know if a single evil spirit can, at the same time, possess more than one body. If they can only possess one body at a time, then there were about two thousand evil spirits in the man (see Mark 5:13).

When liberated from the evil spirits, the man was normal, clothed, and "in his right mind."

Just as a passing note, the reaction of the herd of swine when the evil spirits entered into them was to run violently down the hill and drown themselves in the sea rather than turn their bodies over to evil spirits. Yet so many people today seem to do all they can (violating the commandments) to invite evil spirits into their bodies.

There is another example in the life of the Savior that causes us to question the depth of our understanding about evil spirits.

> And one of the multitude answered and said, Master, I have brought unto thee my son, which hath a dumb spirit;
>
> And wheresoever he taketh him, he teareth him: and he foameth, and gnasheth with his teeth, and pineth away: and I spake to thy disciples that they should cast him out; and they could not.
>
> He answereth him, and saith, O faithless generation, how long shall I be with you? how long shall I suffer you? bring him unto me.
>
> And they brought him unto him: and when he saw him, straightway the spirit tare him; and he fell on the ground, and wallowed foaming.
>
> And he asked his father, How long is it ago since this came unto him? And he said, Of a child.
>
> And ofttimes it hath cast him into the fire, and into the waters, to destroy him: but if thou canst do any thing, have compassion on us, and help us.
>
> Jesus said unto him, If thou canst believe, all things *are* possible to him that believeth.
>
> And straightway the father of the child cried out, and said with tears, Lord, I believe; help thou mine unbelief.
>
> When Jesus saw that the people came running together, he rebuked the foul spirit, saying unto him, *Thou* dumb and deaf spirit, I charge thee, come out of him, and enter no more into him.
>
> And *the spirit* cried, and rent him sore, and came out of him: and he was as one dead; insomuch that many said, He is dead.
>
> But Jesus took him by the hand, and lifted him up; and he arose.
>
> And when he was come into the house, his disciples asked him privately, Why could not we cast him out?
>
> And he said unto them, **This kind can come forth by nothing, but by prayer and fasting.**" (Mark 9:17–29)

Our objective is not to try to explore the different kinds of evil spirits only to note that all evil spirits are not the same and some require greater means to dislodge them. To the Saints in our day, the Lord said,

> For I am God, and mine arm is not shortened; and I will show miracles, signs, and wonders, unto all those who believe on my name.
>
> And whoso shall ask it in my name in faith, **they shall cast out devils**; they shall heal the sick; they shall cause the blind to receive their sight, and the deaf to hear, and the dumb to speak, and the lame to walk.

> And the time speedily cometh that great things are to be shown forth unto the children of men. (D&C 35:8–10)

Without constant vigilance, we may fall into the trap like Korihor, the anti-Christ of the Book of Mormon (see Alma 30). After being struck dumb by the Lord for asking for a sign, Korihor said,

> But behold, the devil hath deceived me; for he appeared unto me in the form of an angel, and said unto me: Go and reclaim this people, for they have all gone astray after an unknown God. And he said unto me: There is no God; yea, and he taught me that which I should say. And I have taught his words; and I taught them because they were pleasing unto the carnal mind; and I taught them, even until I had much success, insomuch that I verily believed that they were true; and for this cause I withstood the truth, even until I have brought this great curse upon me. (Alma 30:53)

The devil can appear as an angel, his message is pleasing to the carnal mind, and he will assist those he deceives to have great success—for a time. Then, when they are beyond the point of no return, he rips the rug from beneath them and laughs as they plunge into outer darkness. Mormon makes this sobering observation:

> And thus we see the end of him who perverteth the ways of the Lord; and thus we see that the devil will not support his children at the last day, but doth speedily drag them down to hell. (Alma 30:60)

Without the help of the Savior, mortality becomes a nightmare. Were it not for the Savior's sacrifice, Jacob, in the Book of Mormon, described our inescapable fate:

> And our spirits must have become like unto him, and we become devils, angels to a devil, to be shut out from the presence of our God, and to remain with the father of lies, in misery, like unto himself; yea, to that being who beguiled our first parents, who transformeth himself nigh unto an angel of light, and stirreth up the children of men unto secret combinations of murder and all manner of secret works of darkness. (2 Nephi 9:9)

It definitely is time to take a step back and see if Satan, who has the ability to "transform himself nigh unto an angel of light" is deceiving us with his subtle tactics.

CHAPTER 12

When a Great One Stumbles

It seems that I hear more frequently now than in previous times that people who have been pillars in their wards or stakes no longer associate with the Church. What happened? At what point did their faith start to wane and disbelief take its place? Perhaps if we could determine that, we could also use that starting point to protect ourselves from being deceived.

The Prophet Joseph Smith gave us this key:

> I will give you one of the Keys of the mysteries of the Kingdom. It is an eternal principle, that has existed with God from all eternity: That man who rises up to condemn others, finding fault with the Church, saying that they are out of the way, while he himself is righteous, then know assuredly, that that man is in the high road to apostasy; and if he does not repent, will apostatize, as God lives. The principle is as correct as the one that Jesus put forth in saying that he who seeketh a sign is an adulterous person; and that principle is eternal, undeviating, and firm as the pillars of heaven; for whenever you see a man seeking after a sign, you may set it down that he is an adulterous man. (*Teachings of the Prophet Joseph Smith*, 156–57)

It is clear that the Church is made up of imperfect people. Even if a Perfect Person (Christ) were to come among us, many would find fault with Him. After performing a number of miracles, there was still a division among the people concerning Christ. John records,

> There was a division therefore again among the Jews for these sayings.
>
> And many of them said, He hath a devil, and is mad; why hear ye him?

> Others said, These are not the words of him that hath a devil. Can a devil open the eyes of the blind? (John 10:19–21)

Concerning the weaknesses and faults in people, it seems to be true that "you will see what you look for." Marriages are weakened and destroyed because one or both of the partners begin to look for the faults in the other. Friendships are blown asunder because we look for ulterior motives to the actions of those we formerly have trusted. Often years later and when reconciliation is no longer possible, we discover that what we thought we saw was not reality. A lifetime of bitterness and hatred has robbed us of many wonderful experiences and memories.

Are wrongs real at times? Absolutely. The Lord warned over 2000 years ago, "Woe unto the world because of offences! for it must needs be that offences come; but woe to that man by whom the offence cometh!" (Matthew 18:7). Opportunities to be offended will be frequent and often come from people or events you least expect.

Then it isn't so much that occasions to be offended will come. It is more important how you respond to those offenses. Once again, the Prophet Joseph Smith gives some timely advice:

> O ye Twelve! and all Saints! profit by this important Key—that in all your trials, troubles, temptations, afflictions, bonds, imprisonments and death, see to it, that you do not betray heaven; that you do not betray Jesus Christ; that you do not betray the brethren; that you do not betray the revelations of God, whether in Bible, Book of Mormon, or Doctrine and Covenants, or any other that ever was or ever will be given and revealed unto man in this world or that which is to come. Yea, in all your kicking and flounderings, see to it that you do not this thing, lest innocent blood be found upon your skirts, and you go down to hell. All other sins are not to be compared to sinning against the Holy Ghost, and proving a traitor to the brethren. (*Teachings of the Prophet Joseph Smith*, 156)

A number of years ago, I met a good friend who, to my surprise, no longer considered himself a member of the Church. This man had held responsible priesthood positions and had been a pillar in his ward. We talked for some time, and he shared the reasons he'd fallen away from the Church. He said that after his release from being bishop, people acted as though he didn't exist. No one greeted him each week when he attended meetings. Nobody ask for his advice. His family, who used to be the center of the hub of activities for the youth, seemed to be ostracized.

As the weeks and months passed, he began to see flaws in the way his replacement conducted meetings, called and released people, and conducted the affairs of the ward. He said that over time his attendance at meetings became more sporadic. No one seemed to care that he wasn't a regular attender. He and his family started going on picnics and outings during Church time. At first the children questioned him but soon found their new found freedom more exciting than "boring Church meetings." Often their outings centered around boating or swimming, so he and his wife no longer wore their garments. Eventually that evolved into never wearing their garments.

He spoke about listening to general conference (which we used to attend together) and how the talks of the Brethren and leaders were old, stale, repetitive, and irrelevant. Before long, he started listening to what the "anti-Mormons" were saying. He decided to investigate their claims. To his amazement, they seemed to have "incontrovertible proof" that certain leaders were living a double standard and that some doctrine was being misrepresented. And the list went on.

Before long, he discussed with his wife their lack of faith in the Church and its teachings. They made application to have their names removed from the records of the Church. He said that many Church leaders met with him and his wife to try to get them to realize what they were doing and to come back into the fold—all to no avail. They had made up their minds.

When I spoke with him, it had been several years since they had left the Church. He said they were the happiest years of their lives. No longer did they feel the pressure to be perfect, to keep the commandments, and to deny themselves of the pleasures of the world.

He asked me how I justified his current enjoyment of life with his former stress as a bishop. After some thought, I told him it was a "no brainer." He and his wife no longer posed a threat to Satan and his kingdom. They were no longer candidates for the celestial kingdom and had cancelled the claim they had on each other and their children. He seemed shocked. He hadn't thought of it that way before.

We parted friends after our lengthy discussion. I told him I'd like to keep in touch. He agreed because we had enjoyed many memorable activities for many years. However, in spite of our commitment, I didn't hear from him for another five years. When I did it was a frantic plea for help.

I drove the several hours to where he lived and met with him at the time and place we'd agreed upon. As I sat in the restaurant awaiting his arrival, the appointed time passed. I turned around to see if I had missed him. My eye caught hold of an aged man who looked like his world had crushed him to ashes. He was unshaven, unkempt, dejected, and the epitome of one who had fallen on hard times. There was just a glimmer of recognition. I moved to his table.

He said he had arrived early but couldn't bring himself to joining me. He was afraid that I'd walk away from him. I gave him a hug and we sat down to talk. He told me what was obvious from his countenance. His marriage had fallen apart. He had violated his marital covenants. His wife had divorced him. His children had turned on him. He had been fired from his job. His "drinking buddies" had turned their backs on him. He felt he had passed the point of no return and had seriously contemplated taking his own life. That was when he had frantically called me.

Through his uncontrolled sobs, he lamented that the only real and lasting happiness he had enjoyed was when his family was fully engaged in the Church. He asked if I thought it was possible for him to get back into the Church. I assured him that it was but that it likely wouldn't be easy. I asked him about his proof of the corruption of Church leaders and his incontrovertible proof about the falseness of the doctrine. He made a statement that I have alluded to earlier in the chapter: "You see what you are looking for." All of the mass of anti-Mormon "crap" was just that—crap.

Then he pointed out what brought me to the point of this chapter. He said, "I never took the time to ask myself, 'What am I getting in exchange for giving up everything the Church offers?'" He admitted that he was smart enough to recognize that the "fun and games" of the world were temporary and fleeting while the promises of the Church had eternal implications. But he rationalized in the beginning of his apostasy that in the back of his mind he thought he could sample the "good things" of the world for a time and then retreat to the safety of the Church. He said he thought he could have the "best of both worlds."

It wasn't until he was deeply engrossed in the ways of the world that he realized that the desire to return to the Church wasn't strong enough to overcome the lure of the world. He said that it wasn't until after our meeting five years previously that his illusionary world began to crumble.

I asked if it might be possible to reconcile with his wife, who I knew he adored. He said his wife had come to him shortly after our meeting and said she wanted to get back into the Church. When he objected and she continued to pressure him, he turned his affections to another woman. That escalated to the divorce and the destruction of his family. Now his wife has married a wonderful man in the Church. She had been rebaptized and was seeking a cancellation of sealings so that her and the kids could be sealed to the new husband.

Not to make this chapter too long, let me say that over the next while, with frequent phone conversations, visits, and encouragement, he did turn his life around and has been rebaptized. He is awaiting word on the restoration of his priesthood and temple blessings. He hasn't remarried but is gaining more confidence as he sees members of the Church embrace him and not condemn him because of his past.

If you find yourself teetering in your testimony, ask yourself the question my friend asked me: "What am I gaining for what I am contemplating giving up?" You will discover that the Lord's admonition "Be still and know that I am God" (D&C 101:16) holds a key to continued Church activity. In those quiet moments when the world or its influence isn't bombarding you with promises it can never keep, that still, small voice helps you keep things in proper eternal perspective. As you remember the multitude of spiritual experiences you may have had in the past, and the joy you felt as you participated in sacred ordinances, reading the scriptures, and spending time in solemn prayer, your resolve to keep holding tightly to the iron rod will be increased. You will feel the love and concern of the Savior and know more surely than ever that Heavenly Father really is willing to be involved in the details of your life—if you will allow Him to be.

CHAPTER 13

Satan's Primary Targets: The Body, Marriage, and Family

If you are a list-maker, you know that your top priority tasks for the day are written on a note pad, with the most important duty being listed as number one and those of lesser importance numerically listed below it. Your first concern is to tackle number one and then move down the list as time permits.

Using that same logic, we should be able to prioritize Satan's primary areas of focus in his relentless efforts to destroy. Heavenly Father's plan for the progress and eventual exaltation of His children has the following sequential necessities:

1. Get a physical body

Why do we need a physical body? Because in order to become like God, we must have a physical body. Joseph Smith wrote,

> The Father has a body of flesh and bones as tangible as man's; the Son also; but the Holy Ghost has not a body of flesh and bones, but is a personage of Spirit. Were it not so, the Holy Ghost could not dwell in us. (D&C 130:22)

2. Develop faith in Christ and His gospel

We must learn what the covenant path is and then willingly following it by repenting of our sins. An angel explained to King Benjamin:

> And moreover, I say unto you, that there shall be no other name given nor any other way nor means whereby salvation can come unto the children of men, only in and through the name of Christ, the Lord Omnipotent. (Mosiah 3:17)

3. Be baptized and receive the Holy Ghost

Receiving the Holy Ghost is the gate to the straight and narrow path leading to the celestial presence of God and receiving the crown of eternal life. Nephi taught,

> Wherefore, do the things which I have told you I have seen that your Lord and your Redeemer should do; for, for this cause have they been shown unto me, that ye might know the gate by which ye should enter. For the gate by which ye should enter is repentance and baptism by water; and then cometh a remission of your sins by fire and by the Holy Ghost.
>
> And then are ye in this strait and narrow path which leads to eternal life; yea, ye have entered in by the gate; ye have done according to the commandments of the Father and the Son; and ye have received the Holy Ghost, which witnesses of the Father and the Son, unto the fulfilling of the promise which he hath made, that if ye entered in by the way ye should receive. (2 Nephi 31:17–18)

4. Enter the temple

You must enter the temple to receive the ordinances of exaltation. For man, he must first be faithful enough to obtain the Melchizedek Priesthood and magnify his calling, which has (in part) the following blessings:

> For whoso is faithful unto the obtaining these two priesthoods of which I have spoken, and the magnifying their calling, are **sanctified by the Spirit unto the renewing of their bodies**. . . .
>
> And he that receiveth my Father receiveth my Father's kingdom; therefore **all that my Father hath shall be given unto him.** (D&C 84:33, 38. See verses 33–41 for the entire oath and covenant of the priesthood.)

This is the promise the Lord gives as we enter the temple to receive our endowments:

> For behold, I have prepared a great endowment and blessing to be poured out upon them, inasmuch as they are faithful and continue in humility before me. (D&C 105:12)

5. ENTER INTO THE NEW AND EVERLASTING COVENANT OF MARRIAGE

As baptism is the key that opens the doors of the celestial kingdom (see John 3:3–5), so eternal marriage is the key to open the door to the highest degree of the celestial kingdom.

> In the celestial glory there are three heavens or degrees;
>
> And in order to obtain the highest, a man must enter into this order of the priesthood [meaning the new and everlasting covenant of marriage];
>
> And if he does not, he cannot obtain it.
>
> He may enter into the other, but that is the end of his kingdom; he cannot have an increase. (D&C 131:1–4)

6. ENDURE TO THE END

Nephi had this requirement confirmed by both the Father and the Son:

> And I heard a voice from the Father, saying: Yea, the words of my Beloved are true and faithful. He that endureth to the end, the same shall be saved.
>
> And now, my beloved brethren, I know by this that unless a man shall endure to the end, in following the example of the Son of the living God, he cannot be saved. (2 Nephi 31:15–16)

Then Nephi followed up with this declaration:

> Wherefore, ye must press forward with a steadfastness in Christ, having a perfect brightness of hope, and a love of God and of all men. Wherefore, if ye shall press forward, feasting upon the word of Christ, and endure to the end, behold, thus saith the Father: Ye shall have eternal life. (2 Nephi 31:20)

Given that priority list of the requirements for eternal life, and knowing that "the devil is an enemy unto God, and fighteth against him continually, and inviteth and enticeth to sin, and to do that which is evil continually" (Moroni 7:12), it should be obvious where Satan will focus his efforts to destroy mankind.

First, he will try to prevent a spirit son or daughter of God from getting a physical body. So effective has he been in convincing the masses that a woman has the "right to choose" whether to have the baby that she, through exercising her agency to engage in life-creating activities, has created, that laws allowing abortion have been passed. Too bad (for Satan) that he doesn't realize what the Lord taught Joseph Smith, "And I also beheld that all children who die before they arrive at the years of accountability are saved in the celestial kingdom of heaven" (D&C 137:10; see also Mosiah 15:25).

If Satan cannot prevent a child from being born, he will then do all in his power to destroy that person through the abuse of their body, the evil acts of others, or the diseases brought on by breaking the commandments of God.

The power of procreation has been gifted to man by God on a trial basis. If we learn to control our passions and use that power in the way God has outlined, then it will be returned to us as resurrected beings. If we abuse it, we run the risk of losing that power as part of our resurrected bodies. Paul taught, "Flee fornication. Every sin that a man doeth is without the body; but he that committeth fornication sinneth against his own body" (1 Corinthians 6:18). It is obvious how successful Satan has been in getting mankind to disregard the law of chastity.

Since "marriage is ordained of God" (see " The Family: A Proclamation to the World"), Satan has succeeded in convincing people that "cohabitation" is better than marriage. For those Latter-day Saints who have been taught all their lives that marriage in the temple is the God-ordained way of marriage, Satan tries (with some degree of success) to get LDS couples to marry civilly with the idea that "eventually" they will be sealed in the temple. They consciously walk away from the endowment of power promised in the sealing ceremony. Thus, they try to outwit Satan with their limited knowledge and power. Far too many couples never follow through on their commitment to marry in the temple, or they postpone their temple marriage for many, many years.

Read this sobering declaration given by the Lord concerning those who choose to have a civil marriage rather than a temple marriage:

> Therefore, if a man marry him a wife in the world, and he marry her not by me nor by my word, and he covenant with her so long as he is in the world and she with him, their covenant and marriage are not of force when they are dead, and when they are out of the world; therefore, they are not bound by any law when they are out of the world.
>
> Therefore, when they are out of the world they neither marry nor are given in marriage; but are appointed angels in heaven, which angels are

> ministering servants, to minister for those who are worthy of a far more, and an exceeding, and an eternal weight of glory.
>
> For these angels did not abide my law; therefore, they cannot be enlarged, but remain separately and singly, without exaltation, in their saved condition, to all eternity; and from henceforth are not gods, but are angels of God forever and ever. (D&C 132:15–17)

Since marriage from the very beginning of man's mortal existence has been defined by God as being between a man and a woman (see Genesis 2:24–25), Satan has now clouded the issue by promoting marriage between two people of the same gender. There are many other perversions in the sexual relations of men and women that testify to the fact that Satan is fighting continually against God in everything necessary for mankind to gain eternal life.

Missionaries in particular, but anyone who has tried to help people prepare for baptism, can readily attest that Satan seldom allows nonmembers to investigate and join the Church without his devilish attempts to dissuade them. If he fails to prevent the baptism, he continues to encourage them to discontinue activity in the Church. The number of converts who "come in the front door and exit the back door" of the Church demonstrates how effective Satan is.

If a couple marries in the temple, the fight is not over. Satan does all in his power to divide the husband from the wife, knowing that marriage in the temple is a "trilateral" covenant between husband and wife and God. Temple marriage is like a triangle, with God at the top and the husband and wife occupying the lower two corners. Satan knows that a trilateral covenant cannot endure with only bilateral involvement. For example, if a wife does all she can to make the marriage work, including God in her prayers and thoughts, but the husband does not join the effort, the marriage is destined to fail. If both the husband and wife choose to engage in activities that distance themselves from God, they cannot have an enduring relationship. John described God as "Love" (1 John 4:16). If God is excluded from the relationship, then love dwindles and eventually dies. As long as the husband is progressing and becoming more like God, and the wife is doing the same, then they become closer to each other as they approach being godlike.

Enduring to the end seems like a daunting task. It is if you try to do it all at once; however, one day at a time enduring faithfully to the end is very doable.

How do you know if you are successfully enduring? Three things must happen to all ordinances in order for them to be in effect after death:

1. The ordinances must be "made"

2. They must be "entered into"

3. They must be "sealed by the Holy Spirit of Promise" (see D&C 132:7)

How does one "make" a covenant? Baptism provides a good example. The candidate goes down into the water. One having authority pronounces the prescribed words, puts the candidate under the water, and brings him up again. The covenant is made.

How does one "enter into" a covenant? By doing what he promised to do. For instance, a person who is baptized covenanted to be "willing to mourn with those that mourn; yea, and comfort those that stand in need of comfort, and to stand as witnesses of God at all times and in all things, and in all places that [they] may be in, even until death" (Mosiah 18:9).

What does it mean and how can one tell if they are "sealed by the Holy Spirit of Promise?" If you break down the phrase in question, you see the Lord is speaking of "the Holy Spirit" or Holy Ghost operating in his office as a witness testifying that the conditions of the covenant are being successfully lived. Therefore, promising that, if the person continues in the course he is pursuing, the promised blessing will be his. As long as the Holy Spirit is evident in the person's life, it is the assurance that, although not perfect, he is just or justified—being without divine condemnation. If the Holy Spirit does not continue to dwell with the covenant maker, it is a warning that unless corrections are made in the way the covenant is being lived, the promised blessing will not be forthcoming.

Satan will always tell you that you are not good enough to qualify for eternal life because you are not yet perfect. However, the presence of the Spirit is Heavenly Father's way of letting us know that we are headed in the right direction and are moving ahead as quickly as He requires of us to qualify for eternal life. The Lord revealed, "And the place where it is my will that you should tarry, for the main, shall be signalized unto you by the **peace** and **power of my Spirit**, that shall flow unto you" (D&C 111:8).

When a person learns to recognize the presence of the Spirit, not necessarily the intense feelings associated with a peak experience, but that calm, peaceful feeling, he can resist Satan's lies about his unworthiness. Paul speaks of the inner peace that passes all understanding (see Philippians 4:7). When you recognize those two conditions in your life (peace and the Spirit), then you know that "for the main" (or, in other words, you are heading in the right direction) you are acceptable to God.

You be the judge. If you are in step with God's required outline to gain eternal life, don't let the adversary convince you otherwise. He was a liar from the beginning and is still a liar (see D&C 93:25). Listening to him is a sure formula to be deceived and discouraged.

CHAPTER 14

One Slip-Up Does Not Signal Eternal Failure

We all make mistakes or sin. Paul stated, "For all have sinned, and come short of the glory of God" (Romans 3:23). Satan would have you believe that you are the only one who has stumbled on the pathway to eternal glory. Consider Peter, Christ's chief Apostle. He denied even knowing the Savior three times in one night. Yet the Savior knew of his goodness and his potential and restored him to his position as President of the Church following His ascension.

Paul, originally named Saul, had a misplaced enthusiasm fighting against the newly organized Christian Church. Luke records, "AND Saul, yet breathing out threatenings and slaughter against the disciples of the Lord, went unto the high priest" (Acts 9:1) and got arrest warrants against the Saints, persecuting and imprisoning them. The Lord straightened him out by a direct vision, and he became the most powerful missionary in the post resurrection era. How did he handle his past, which Satan surely threw in his face on a daily basis? He tells it himself, which is instructive for you and me when Satan tries his destructive tactics against us.

> Brethren, I count not myself to have apprehended: **but *this* one thing *I do*, forgetting those things which are behind, and reaching forth unto those things which are before,**
>
> **I press toward the mark for the prize of the high calling of God in Christ Jesus.** (Philippians 3:13–14)

Alma and the Sons of Mosiah were, by Alma's own account, the "vilest of all sinners" (see Mosiah 28:4), yet they became the greatest missionaries in the Book of Mormon. They were instruments in the hands of the Lord and converted thousands of the Lamanites to the Church.

Joseph Smith allowed Martin Harris to take the 116 manuscript pages containing the Book of Lehi after soliciting the Lord three times. The first two requests were denied. Martin subsequently lost the manuscript. You may not think that was terribly serious since the Lord had made provisions to replace it over 2500 years before. However, on closer analysis, Joseph's choice deprived the entire world of a book of scripture from then to the Second Coming. Not a small thing. If the Lord forgave Joseph Smith, He can and will forgive you.

This is part of a revelation the Lord gave to Joseph Smith after he had lost the manuscript pages:

> And behold, how oft you have transgressed the commandments and the laws of God, and have gone on in the persuasions of men.
>
> For, behold, you should not have feared man more than God. Although men set at naught the counsels of God, and despise his words—
>
> Yet you should have been faithful; and he would have extended his arm and supported you against all the fiery darts of the adversary; and he would have been with you in every time of trouble.
>
> Behold, thou art Joseph, and thou wast chosen to do the work of the Lord, but because of transgression, if thou art not aware thou wilt fall.
>
> **But remember, God is merciful; therefore, repent of that which thou hast done which is contrary to the commandment which I gave you, and thou art still chosen, and art again called to the work;**
>
> **Except thou do this** [repent and get your act together]**, thou shalt be delivered up and become as other men, and have no more gift.** (D&C 3:6–11)

You may say, "Well that is good, but I'm no Joseph Smith!" However, the Lord said, "What I say unto one I say unto all; pray always lest that wicked one have power in you, and remove you out of your place" (D&C 93:49).

You may have some wonderful promises in your patriarchal blessing. Satan will tell you that if you have sinned, especially more serious sins, that you have disqualified yourself from receiving those blessings. That is as false as any of his other lies.

Some of the greatest counsel concerning sinners and repentance, as well as a righteous people who turn to iniquity, is found in the Old Testament. Read carefully what Ezekiel wrote:

> Therefore, O thou son of man, speak unto the house of Israel; Thus ye speak, saying, If our transgressions and our sins *be* upon us, and we pine away in them, how should we then live?
>
> Say unto them, *As* I live, saith the Lord GOD, I have no pleasure in the death of the wicked; but that the wicked turn from his way and live: turn ye, turn ye from your evil ways; for why will ye die, O house of Israel?
>
> Therefore, thou son of man, say unto the children of thy people, The righteousness of the righteous shall not deliver him in the day of his transgression: as for the wickedness of the wicked, he shall not fall thereby in the day that he turneth from his wickedness; neither shall the righteous be able to live for his *righteousness* in the day that he sinneth.
>
> When I shall say to the righteous, *that* he shall surely live; if he trust to his own righteousness, and commit iniquity, all his righteousnesses shall not be remembered; but for his iniquity that he hath committed, he shall die for it.
>
> Again, when I say unto the wicked, Thou shalt surely die; if he turn from his sin, and do that which is lawful and right;
>
> *If* the wicked restore the pledge, give again that he had robbed, walk in the statutes of life, without committing iniquity; he shall surely live, he shall not die.
>
> None of his sins that he hath committed shall be mentioned unto him: he hath done that which is lawful and right; he shall surely live. (Ezekiel 33:10–16)

Now is definitely the right day to take stock of where you are spiritually and begin the repentance process. Every day you wait to get right with the Lord is one day less you have to complete the process and do those things you know in your heart you want to do before the night closes in on your mortal stay.

If you need a place to start the repentance process, take an inventory of those things you may have done that have put you at odds with the Lord and His Church. Commit to keep the Word of Wisdom, the law of chastity, and other commandments you may be currently violating. Next, start doing those things the prophets and apostles have counseled: read the scriptures daily (maybe best to start with the Book of Mormon). Begin the practice of daily prayer. Start attending Church (this may be difficult if you have been away for some time).

You may mistakenly think that everyone at Church is looking at you and knows your sinful past. That certainly isn't the case. Many Saints will be there to welcome you back and help you feel comfortable in Church meetings. Under the current program, sacrament meetings last one hour and alternating Priesthood/Relief Society and Sunday School last fifty minutes.

Then find out who the ward executive secretary is and make an appointment to see the bishop. Be humble and teachable. Whatever the bishop counsels you to do, do it. Be consistent in your efforts to change. You likely won't be perfect all at once, but step-by-step, you will see rapid improvement in the way you feel about yourself and life in general. Set realistic goals and, with the help of the bishop, set a target date to rejoin the Church (if your membership has been removed). Get your temple recommend renewed if you are worthy. All of this will invite the Spirit back into your life and create an enthusiasm that may have been lacking for some time.

Understand that if you have been through a disciplinary council, it will require the reconvening of the same level of counsel you appeared before when action was taken against you in order to reinstate you into the Church. Restoring your priesthood (if you were excommunicated) and renewal of your temple recommend will likely require you demonstrating for a year that your repentance is real. Whatever is required, the rewards far outweigh the inconvenience.

This is the counsel and invitation given by the Lord:

> Draw near unto me and I will draw near unto you; seek me diligently and ye shall find me; ask, and ye shall receive; knock, and it shall be opened unto you.
>
> Whatsoever ye ask the Father in my name it shall be given unto you, that is expedient for you. D&C 88:63–64)

Take the Lord at His word: "For I will be merciful to their unrighteousness, and their sins and their iniquities will I remember no more" (Hebrews 8:12).

CHAPTER 15

Difference between How the World Is Tempted and How the Saints Are Tempted

One of Satan's most effective tactics is telling the Saints that they are no better than anyone else. While it is true that we don't view ourselves as superior or above others, it is also true that when the Lord puts upon us his covenants and priesthood, we become a peculiar people. Recall what the Lord said to the children of Israel (of whom you are a part): "For thou *art* an holy people unto the LORD thy God, and the LORD hath chosen thee to be a peculiar people unto himself, above all the nations that *are* upon the earth" (Deuteronomy 14:2). That is the label the Lord put on you—not one you took upon yourself.

What is the difference between you and those who are not yet members of the Church? Seen or unseen, there is a huge difference. The Lord revealed to Joseph Smith,

> And it must needs be that the **devil should tempt the children of men**, or they could not be agents unto themselves; for if they never should have bitter they could not know the sweet—
>
> Wherefore, it came to pass that the devil tempted Adam, and he partook of the forbidden fruit and transgressed the commandment, wherein he became subject to the will of the devil, because he yielded unto temptation. (D&C 29:39–40)

The "children of men" is a term used by the Lord to designate those who would not listen to His word and join the Church (see Moses 8:19–20). Now note the difference in intensity which the devil and his angels attack the members of the Church:

> And while we were yet in the Spirit, the Lord commanded us that we should write the vision; for we beheld Satan, that old serpent, even the devil, who rebelled against God, and sought to take the kingdom of our God and his Christ—
>
> Wherefore, **he maketh war with the saints of God, and encompasseth them round about**.
>
> And we saw a vision of the sufferings of those with whom he made war and overcame. (D&C 76:28–30)

Can you see the difference between "being tempted" and having "war" made against you? Also note that the devil "encompasseth" the Saints round about. Since that is a revealed truth, what area of your life do you think is immune from the buffeting and temptations of the devil?

Why would Satan be so concerned about the Saints—more than the general population of the world? First, the Saints have made covenants with the Lord that open the door to the celestial kingdom (baptism—see John 3:3–5). If the Saints live worthy lives, they can have the Holy Ghost as a constant companion. That Spirit is the key to judge between good and evil. Mormon counseled,

> Wherefore, take heed, my beloved brethren, that ye do not judge that which is evil to be of God, or that which is good and of God to be of the devil.
>
> For behold, my brethren, it is given unto you to judge, that ye may know good from evil; and the way to judge is as plain, that ye may know with a perfect knowledge, as the daylight is from the dark night.
>
> For behold, the **Spirit of Christ** is given to every man, that he may know good from evil; wherefore, I show unto you the way to judge; for every thing which inviteth to do good, and to persuade to believe in Christ, is sent forth by the power and gift of Christ; wherefore ye may know with a perfect knowledge it is of God. (Moroni 7:14–16)

If every person on earth could judge between good and evil and choose good, Satan would have little or no power. It is because of deception that Satan gets most of his power.

> But wo unto them that are deceivers and hypocrites, for, thus saith the Lord, I will bring them to judgment.

> Behold, verily I say unto you, **there are hypocrites among you, who have deceived some, which has given the adversary power;** but behold such shall be reclaimed;
>
> But the hypocrites shall be detected and shall be cut off, either in life or in death, even as I will; and wo unto them who are cut off from my church, for the same are overcome of the world.
>
> Wherefore, let every man beware lest he do that which is not in truth and righteousness before me. (D&C 50:6–9)

In another chapter, we discussed that anyone who will "war the Christian warfare" will have evil spirits and devils to contend with every day. You may mistake (unless you understand) how to interpret those constant temptations. They are actually Satan's way of bearing testimony of the potential harm and threat you pose to him and his kingdom. If you win, he will lose eternally.

I have always loved this statement by George Albert Smith, given in 1857:

> This makes me think of an old Chinese fable. A man travelling through the country came to a large city, very rich and splendid; he looked at it and said to his guide, "This must be a very righteous people, for I can only see but one little devil in this great city."
>
> The guide replied, "You do not understand, sir. This city is so perfectly given up to wickedness, corruption, degradation, and abomination of every kind, that it requires but one devil to keep them all in subjection."
>
> Travelling on a little further, he came to a rugged path and saw an old man trying to get up the hillside, surrounded by seven great, big, coarse-looking devils.
>
> "Why," says the traveller, "This must be a tremendously wicked old man! Only see how many devils there are around him!"
>
> "This," replied the guide, "is the only righteous man in the country; and there are seven of the biggest devils trying to turn him out of his path, and they all cannot do it. (*Journal of Discourses*, 5:363–64)

Satan has little to worry about with the people of the world. No matter how righteous they may be, until they enter the covenant path by being baptized, they are not yet candidates for the celestial kingdom. Who can point them toward the covenant path? Missionaries and faithful members of the Church.

It seems, therefore, that every missionary who is doing his duty has an invisible target on his back. He doesn't see it, but the devil does. It is a marvel that more missionaries are not killed or tempted to give up and return home before completing their assigned missions. Opposition to every righteous effort only certifies of Satan's concern and prompts him to double his efforts to destroy.

Every Prophet from Wilford Woodruff on (and likely those before him) have tried to explain who these latter-day warriors are. I particularly like a statement by President Ezra Taft Benson, which is representative of what all of the prophets have said.

> For nearly six thousand years, God has held you in reserve to make your appearance in the final days before the Second Coming of the Lord. . . . While our generation will be comparable in wickedness to the days of Noah, when the Lord cleansed the earth by flood, there is a major difference this time. It is that God has saved for the final inning some of his strongest children, who will help bear off the Kingdom triumphantly. And that is where you come in, for you are the generation that must be prepared to meet your God.
>
> All through the ages the prophets have looked down through the corridors of time to our day. Billions of the deceased and those yet to be born have their eyes on us. Make no mistake about it—you are a marked generation. There has never been more expected of the faithful in such a short period of time as there is of us. Never before on the face of this earth have the forces of evil and the forces of good been as well organized. Now is the great day of the devil's power, with the greatest mass murderers of all time living among us. But now is also the great day of the Lord's power, with the greatest number ever of priesthood holders on the earth. And the showdown is fast approaching. ("In His Steps," in *Speeches of the Year*, 1979 [Provo: BYU Press, 1980], 59)

Just a little reflection comparing the war with Satan to an athletic contest should help us understand why we are singled out by the adversary. Who do you double and triple team on the opposing team? Not the one who can't hit a basket if left alone on the court. Not the one who double dribbles the ball. You double and triple team the player who can shoot the winning baskets and defeat your team.

If you understand that, you can see that as long as you are on the Lord's team and worthily fulfilling your calling (not only missionaries but every member), you can expect satanic opposition. Then instead of thinking you are bad, realize that just the opposite is true. A good friend said it this way: "Satan don't kick no dead dogs!" (Jack R. Christianson quote).

You may say you are tired of being kicked around by Satan. As far as I can determine, there are only two means of escape: (1) You can die and go to the spirit world and continue your work there where Satan has no control over the righteous; or (2) You can sin and disqualify yourself from being on the Lord's first team. Other than that, "Buck up buttercup!" It isn't going to get any better until the Second Coming!

Remind yourself often that you were not reserved for this day to fail. With the help of the Savior, you cannot fail. "I can do all things through Christ which strengtheneth me" (Philippians 4:13).

CHAPTER 16

Discouragement and Depression—Satan's Powerful Tools

Caution needs to be exercised when discussing depression. If your depression has a medical cause, then following the suggested practices that follow may not completely relieve the symptoms. However, none of the suggestions in this chapter will be harmful no matter the source of the depression or discouragement.

George Q. Cannon, counselor to four Church Presidents taught,

> Do not allow darkness and gloom to enter into your hearts. I want to give you a rule by which you may know that the spirit which you have is the right spirit. The Spirit of God produces cheerfulness, joy, light, and good feelings. Whenever you feel gloomy and despondent and are downcast, unless it be for your sins, you may know it is not the Spirit of God which you have. **Fight against it and drive it out of your heart. The Spirit of God is a spirit of hope; it is not a spirit of gloom.** (*Deseret Weekly*, January 14, 1897, 48:351)

President Cannon clearly differentiates between the Spirit of God and the depressive spirit. Since Alma calls the plan of salvation the "great plan of happiness" (see Alma 42:8), I am convinced that God's desires for His spirit children is not one of gloom and doom but joy and happiness while traveling the pathway of mortality. The above quote suggests that we need to take a proactive approach to control the negative spirit. Note the one exception President Cannon gives for feeling gloomy and despondent and downcast—our sins! That re-emphasizes the maxim: You can't do bad and feel good.

Since our eternal objective is to become like God, Heber C. Kimball, counselor to Brigham Young gives us a statement to ponder. He said,

> I am perfectly satisfied that my Father and my God is a cheerful, pleasant, lively, and good-natured Being. Why? Because I am cheerful, pleasant, lively, and good-natured when I have His Spirit. That is one reason why I know; and another is—the Lord said, through Joseph Smith, "I delight in a glad heart and a cheerful countenance" [D&C 59:15]. That arises from the perfection of His attributes; He is a jovial, lively person, and a beautiful man. (*Journal of Discourses*, 4:222)

Lehi had as many reasons to be discouraged and depressed as any mortal. However, under the inspiration of Heaven, he wrote, "Adam fell that men might be; and **men are, that they might have joy**" (2 Nephi 2:25). Can a person be depressed or discouraged and still experience joy? Can a person experience happiness and at the same time be battling depression and discouragement? It may require some serious introspection and reflection to determine the answer to those questions.

Joseph Smith had more than his share of depressors. However, he taught,

> **Happiness is the object and design of our existence**; and will be the end thereof, if we pursue the path that leads to it; and this path is virtue, uprightness, faithfulness, holiness, and keeping all the commandments of God. But we cannot keep all the commandments without first knowing them, and we cannot expect to know all, or more than we now know unless we comply with or keep those we have already received. (*Teachings of the Prophet Joseph Smith*, 255)

The first and sure way of taking control of your mental state is to turn to the Savior. He said,

> Therefore, fear not, little flock; do good; let earth and hell combine against you, for if ye are built upon my rock, they cannot prevail.
>
> Behold, I do not condemn you; go your ways and sin no more; perform with soberness the work which I have commanded you.
>
> Look unto me in every thought; doubt not, fear not. (D&C 6:34–36)

During His mortal ministry He said, "I will not leave you comfortless: I will come to you" (John 14:18).

Trust that the Savior will keep His promise. Too often the depressed and discouraged feel like they are all alone. Exercise your faith in Christ and diligently watch for the fulfillment of His promise.

Combining the suggestions from the above quotes and adding a few ideas to ponder, let's proactively drive out the spirit of gloom and doom. From my own and the reported experience of thousands of students and people I have counseled, it seems the sooner one can recognize they are struggling to control the feelings of negativity the easier it is to take steps to reverse the course their spirit is taking. Those who report that the longer they tried to ignore the descending spiral their spirit was taking, the more difficult it was to climb out of the depressive pit.

The mental stance they (the depressed or discouraged) took was also a major factor in how quickly they were able to "snap out of it." If they adopted the "woe is me" attitude, the blessed relief was postponed. If they adopted the attitude that "this is another opportunity to develop my mental and spiritual muscles" and "this is a challenge not a life destroying catastrophe," then recovery was accelerated.

Moroni made an observation that we need to consider: "And if ye have no hope ye must needs be in despair; and despair cometh because of iniquity" (Moroni 10:22). Certainly, sin drives away the Spirit of God. We should note, however, that iniquity is not the only reason someone experiences despair. Without getting down on yourself, do a "reality check." Are there commandments you know you are breaking? Are there commandments you know you are not obeying? None of us is perfect, and the "enemy of all righteousness" will always confront us with our shortcomings. However, let the Lord tell you where you need to improve to rid yourself of the despair that comes from disobedience. "Let us therefore, as many as be perfect, be thus minded: and if in any thing ye be otherwise minded, God shall reveal even this unto you" (Philippians 3:15).

Another often-reported pitfall by those I have counseled is negative self-talk. It seems that we become whatever we tell ourselves that we are. So, starting right now, avoid ALL negative self-talk. Instead of saying, "I'm a bad person," turn it around and say, "I have things I need to change, and with the help of Christ, I can and will overcome them." See the difference in the feeling associated with each statement?

One of the antidotes frequently mentioned as being most helpful in "driving out" the negative spirit is to forget self and serve others. President Hinckley's father's response to Gordon's discouragement as a new missionary and desire to return home has become a classic: "Dear Gordon, I have your recent letter. I have only one suggestion: forget yourself and go to work." Advice obviously taken, and look at the results! If you find yourself thinking too much about yourself, then the light God gave you to lead others to Christ is focused in your own eyes. Then instead of life's challenges being stepping stones toward exaltation, they become stumbling blocks leading to disappointment and despair.

The Lord gives timely counsel in times of discouragement:

> Verily, verily, I say unto you, ye are little children, and ye have not as yet understood how great blessings the Father hath in his own hands and prepared for you;
>
> **And ye cannot bear all things now; nevertheless, be of good cheer, for I will lead you along.** The kingdom is yours and the blessings thereof are yours, and the riches of eternity are yours.
>
> And he who receiveth all things with thankfulness shall be made glorious; and the things of this earth shall be added unto him, even an hundred fold, yea, more. (D&C 78:17–19)

It seems apparent from that scripture that in spite of the fact that we are not going to be able to be 100 percent successful in passing the tests of life, we are to "be of good cheer." Reiterating what He said that was quoted earlier: "I will not leave you comfortless" (John 14:18).

Too often it seems that we engage in activities that invite the dark spirit rather than the Spirit of God. The Lord revealed this test to determine if what you are doing, watching, or participating in has His divine approval:

> And that which doth not edify is not of God, and is darkness.
>
> That which is of God is light; and he that receiveth light, and continueth in God, receiveth more light; and that light groweth brighter and brighter until the perfect day.
>
> And again, verily I say unto you, and I say it that you may know the truth, that you may **chase darkness from among you.** (D&C 50:21–25)

To "edify" is defined as "to instruct in such a way as to improve, enlighten, or uplift morally, spiritually, or intellectually" (*Webster's New World Dictionary*, 4th edition [New York City: Simon & Schuster/Pocket Books, 2003]).

Returning to Joseph Smith's formula for finding lasting happiness, he said we can have it if "we pursue the path that leads to it; and this path is virtue, uprightness, faithfulness, holiness, and keeping all the commandments of God."

Virtue is the very best of everything. *Webster's New World Dictionary* defines virtue as "general moral excellence; right action and thinking; goodness or morality." So, the best associations, the best entertainment, the best practices, the best activities, the best language, and anything liken unto them are virtuous. A quick review of the activities we engage in, entertainment we watch, and language we use may be helpful in identifying areas of needed improvement.

Uprightness is being a person of integrity. Do we do what we say we will do? Can people count on us that our word is as good as a bond? Are we truthful in our business dealings and other commitments we have made? Some serious thought may produce areas that need some fine-tuning to be acceptable to God.

Faithfulness is something every person aspiring to become like God is striving for daily. To a degree, we all fall short of perfection, but when we show by our actions a strong sense of duty or responsibility, we are being faithful.

Holiness is something we all need to work on. The Lord commanded, "Ye shall be holy: for I the LORD your God *am* holy" (Leviticus 19:2). *Webster's New World Dictionary* defines holy as "spiritually perfect or pure; untainted by evil or sin; sinless saintly."

Keeping all the commandments of God. That may seem to disqualify us from the lasting happiness we are seeking, but as the Lord said of the spiritual gifts, "For verily I say unto you, they are given for the benefit of those who love me and keep all my commandments, and **him that seeketh so to do**" (D&C 46:9). As long as you are consciously trying to keep the commandments, you can qualify for the promised happiness.

In answer to the questions asked earlier about being happy if discouraged or depressed. King Benjamin said,

> And moreover, I would desire that ye should consider on the blessed and happy state of those that keep the commandments of God For behold, they are blessed in all things, both temporal and spiritual; and if they hold out faithful to the end they are received into heaven, that thereby they may dwell with God in a state of never-ending happiness. O remember, remember that these things are true; for the Lord God hath spoken it. (Mosiah 2:41)

The key to overcoming the world and finding joy and happiness in this life is to fix our attention on Christ and trust in the promises He has made. Eventually, we will "overcome the world," which the Lord said is His will for us. "For verily I say unto you, I will that ye should overcome the world; wherefore I will have compassion upon you" (D&C 64:2). As you study the scriptures, you will discover that the greatest and most effective antidepressant is the Spirit.

What influence does the Spirit have on us? The Lord said, "Verily, verily, I say unto you, I will impart unto you of my Spirit, which shall enlighten your mind, which shall fill your soul with joy" (D&C 11:13). Follow the formula the Lord has revealed and receive the promised blessings.

CHAPTER 17

Satan's Use of Technology to Entrap

What will be written in this chapter isn't intended to be a judgment or to create a guilt trip but a warning and a heads-up.

The first thing to note is that all of us will someday stand before the judgment bar of God to account for what we have done during our mortal stay.

> And I saw the dead, small and great, stand before God; and the books were opened: and another book was opened, which is *the book* of life: and **the dead were judged out of those things which were written in the books, according to their works**.
>
> And the sea gave up the dead which were in it; and death and hell delivered up the dead which were in them: and **they were judged every man according to their works.** (Revelation 20:12–13)

Where we spend the rest of eternity will be determined in part from what we did while in the probationary state. Amulek urged us not to procrastinate preparing for that judgment day. He taught,

> For behold, this life is the time for men to prepare to meet God; yea, behold **the day of this life is the day for men to perform their labors.**
>
> And now, as I said unto you before, as ye have had so many witnesses, therefore, I beseech of you that ye do not procrastinate the day of your repentance until the end; for after this day of life, which is given us to prepare for eternity, behold, **if we do not improve our time** while in

> this life, then cometh the night of darkness wherein there can be no labor performed. (Alma 34:32–33)

Although none of us knows the time appointed for our exit from mortality, God does. He revealed, "For there is a time appointed for every man, according as his works shall be" (D&C 121:25).

The use of our numbered days here in mortality becomes vitally important. Since Satan is an enemy to God and fighteth against Him continually, wisdom suggests that we be constantly aware of how we use our days. Mormon wrote,

> Wherefore, all things which are good cometh of God; and that which is evil cometh of the devil; for the devil is an enemy unto God, and fighteth against him continually, and inviteth and enticeth to sin, and to do that which is evil continually.
>
> But behold, that which is of God inviteth and enticeth **to do good continually**; wherefore, every thing which inviteth and enticeth to do good, and to love God, and to serve him, is inspired of God. (Moroni 7:12–13)

In considering the marvelous inventions and discoveries God has allowed man to access, it is obvious that initially they were good. Facebook has helped us connect with family and friends who we may have lost contact with years before. However, according to his never-ending efforts to destroy the world (see Moses 4:6), Satan has tempted many to use Facebook in a way that it virtually monopolizes their entire lives. Instagram, Snapchat, Twitter, and other platforms, equally as helpful in the beginning, are now being used to bully, intimidate, and blackmail unsuspecting youth—and many adults. "Selfies" also have been perverted from their original intent into something that can destroy the lives of youth (and adults) to share intimate photos and then in turn have those photos used to coerce the person into immoral activities under the threat of public exposure.

At first, video and internet games were innocent pastimes. As the adversary continues his efforts to destroy, many have become so addicted to "gaming" that marriages have been destroyed, employment has been terminated, family activities have been stopped, and even Church attendance (if attended at all) has become a time to "surf the net," play games, and text friends. Studies have been done about the addictive nature of texting. What, for many, is a valuable tool to communicate with family, business associates and friends has become an activity that preempts conversations, face-to-face interactions, and business transactions. No wonder many businesses have signs instructing people to silence their cell phones while making purchases or transacting business.

The internet is such a valuable tool to access the knowledge of the world. However, as in everything else, Satan has perverted it and tempted evil and designing people to use it to spew filth and pornography to the masses of mankind. How many marriages have been destroyed by one or both spouses viewing pornography? It would be impossible to accurately calculate, but the studies that have been done suggest it is more common than we want to admit. The Lord revealed the negative impact pornography would have on one who continues to view it. "And verily I say unto you, as I have said before, he that looketh on a woman to lust after her, or if any shall commit adultery in their hearts, they shall not have the Spirit, but shall deny the faith and shall fear" (D&C 63:16).

Thousands of years ago, Isaiah saw our day and warned that

> The sinners in Zion are afraid; fearfulness hath surprised the hypocrites. Who among us shall dwell with the devouring fire? who among us shall dwell with everlasting burnings?
>
> He that walketh righteously, and speaketh uprightly; he that despiseth the gain of oppressions, that shaketh his hands from holding of bribes, that **stoppeth his ears from hearing of blood, and shutteth his eyes from seeing evil.** (Isaiah 33:14–15)

"Stopping his ears from hearing of blood" could very well refer to the violence we hear in certain kinds of music and in movies and videos. "Shutting our eyes from seeing evil" could be Isaiah's way of warning us against nudity, immorality, and violence in magazines, on the internet, in videos, and in movies. To "dwell with devouring fire" is descriptive of the burning at the Second Coming. "To dwell with everlasting burnings" is often associated with living with God. That is a definite criteria for escaping the burning at the Second Coming and being suited to dwell eternally with God.

Given that we don't get a "second chance" at successfully passing the tests of mortality once we die, it seems wise to pause and see how we are using our time. Do we spend as much time searching the scriptures and reading the words of living prophets and apostles as we do watching television or surfing the net? Are we so caught up in "gaming" that we have no time to attend the temple or do family history work?

There is yet another area that needs our attention. We are commanded by the Lord to "JUDGE not, that ye be not judged. For with what judgment ye judge, ye shall be judged: and with what measure ye mete, it shall be measured to you again" (Matthew 7:1–2).

Social media has become the platform for people to pass judgment—generally on that which they have little or no knowledge. This was so important that Isaiah again warned us against becoming the judge, jury, and executioner.

> For the terrible one is brought to nought, and the scorner is consumed, and all that watch for iniquity are cut off:
>
> That make a man an offender for a word, and lay a snare for him that reproveth in the gate, and turn aside the just for a thing of nought. (Isaiah 29:20–21)

We are admonished by the Lord:

> But ye are commanded in all things to ask of God, who giveth liberally; and that which the Spirit testifies unto you even so I would that ye should do in all holiness of heart, walking uprightly before me, **considering the end of your salvation**, doing all things with prayer and thanksgiving, that ye may not be seduced by evil spirits, or doctrines of devils, or the commandments of men; for some are of men, and others of devils. (D&C 46:7)

Probably the greatest chapter in scriptures that can act as a PPI (Personal Priesthood Interview) for each of us is Alma 5. If you haven't read that chapter recently, it would be beneficial to pause and read it now. Here is just a part that deals with our future judgment:

> I say unto you, can you imagine to yourselves that ye hear the voice of the Lord, saying unto you, in that day: Come unto me ye blessed, for behold, your works have been the works of righteousness upon the face of the earth?
>
> Or do ye imagine to yourselves that ye can lie unto the Lord in that day, and say—Lord, our works have been righteous works upon the face of the earth—and that he will save you?
>
> Or otherwise, can ye imagine yourselves brought before the tribunal of God with your souls filled with guilt and remorse, having a remembrance of all your guilt, yea, a perfect remembrance of all your wickedness, yea, a remembrance that ye have set at defiance the commandments of God?

> I say unto you, can ye look up to God at that day with a pure heart and clean hands? I say unto you, can you look up, having the image of God engraven upon your countenances?
>
> I say unto you, can ye think of being saved when you have yielded yourselves to become subjects to the devil? (Alma 5:16–20)

As we stand to account for every thought we think, every word we say, and every deed we do wisdom would dictate that we, not social media, take control. In Alma 12:14 we are put on notice:

> For our words will condemn us, yea, all our works will condemn us; we shall not be found spotless; and our thoughts will also condemn us; and in this awful state we shall not dare to look up to our God; and we would fain be glad if we could command the rocks and the mountains to fall upon us to hide us from his presence.

It may not hold much weight when the Lord asks us how we used our time in mortality when we say that we had 50,000 kills on some video game. Like other addictions, those who are being led away carefully down to hell (see 2 Nephi 28: 21) will adamantly insist that they can stop any time they want to. That is a good argument until they try to go "cold turkey." President Nelson and other of our sustained leaders have suggested going a week without social media. From the response many youth gave, it was evident that going for just one week was a serious wake-up call on how addictive social media had become.

Perhaps it would be a worthy challenge for all of us to take President Nelson's challenge and see the difference a week without social media would make. It isn't like we are putting our eternal life in jeopardy by ignoring prophetic counsel—or are we?

CHAPTER 18

Accessing the Limitless Power of the Atonement in Overcoming Satan

Every suggestion in this book has the underlying foundation (either written or implied) that Christ is the key to recognize and overcome Satan. How could He possibly understand the challenges we face in these modern days? Paul gave us the answer when he said,

> For we have not an high priest which cannot be touched with the feeling of our infirmities; but was in all points tempted like as *we are, yet* without sin.
>
> Let us therefore come boldly unto the throne of grace, that we may obtain mercy, and find grace to help in time of need. (Hebrews 4:5–16)

Knowing that Christ was tempted in every single area that any person on earth has been tempted and yet never sinned should give us the confidence that He can help us in our time of trouble. And His "grace" (divine enabling power) is sufficient to help us win over Satan. Remember what He revealed to Joseph Smith: "BEHOLD, and hearken, O ye elders of my church, saith the Lord your God, even Jesus Christ, your advocate, who knoweth the weakness of man and how to succor them who are tempted" (D&C 62:1). Following that, He said, "For verily I say unto you, I will that ye should overcome the world; wherefore I will have compassion upon you" (D&C 64:2).

He will never turn His back on us, no matter how many times we struggle and fall. He promised, "Yea, verily I say unto you, if ye will come unto me ye shall have eternal life. Behold, mine arm of mercy is extended towards you, and whosoever will come, him will I receive; and blessed are those who come unto me" (3 Nephi 9:14).

In addition, the Savior taught that, "These things I have spoken unto you, that in me ye might have peace. In the world ye shall have tribulation: but be of good cheer; I have overcome the world" (John 16:33).

The Lord knew exactly what we would be going through as we sequence, day by day, through mortality. He knew we wouldn't pass all of the tests perfectly. In spite of that, He said to be of good cheer. Perhaps He was saying, "Don't let mortality become a time of gloom and doom. Try turning each challenge into an opportunity to learn and grow."

Consider the implications of this saying attributed to Ghana Airways: "'Christ Is the Answer: What Is the Question?' A Ghana Airways Prayer Vigil and Its Implications for Religion, Evil and Public Space" (J. Kwabena Asamoah-Gyadu, *Journal of Religion in Africa*, Vol. 35, Fasc. 1, New Dimensions in the Study of Pentecostalism [Feb. 2005], 93–117).

How lamentable! We live in the day of fulfillment of the prophesy Amos wrote about thousands of years ago:

> Behold, the days come, saith the Lord GOD, that I will send a famine in the land, not a famine of bread, nor a thirst for water, but of hearing the words of the LORD:
>
> And they shall wander from sea to sea, and from the north even to the east, they shall run to and fro to seek the word of the LORD, and shall not find *it*. (Amos 8:11–12)

But this our day. We may be as essential to the survival of the human race as Queen Esther was in saving the Jews. As her uncle, Mordecai, said to Esther: "Who knoweth whether thou art come to the kingdom for *such* a time as this?" (Esther 4:14).

It may be that we will not see until the next life the fulfillment of this statement, but be assured that as Ammon said this, so you will look back on your mortal experience and say the same thing:

> Yea, I know that I am nothing; as to my strength I am weak; therefore I will not boast of myself, but I will boast of my God, **for in his strength I can do all things**; yea, behold, many mighty miracles we have wrought in this land, for which we will praise his name forever. (Alma 26:12)

You may choose to discount that statement, but remember what President Ezra Taft Benson said of you. You were reserved for 6000 years to fight this final battle with evil. He also said you were among the most noble and strongest sons and daughters of God. Without keeping that vision firmly in our minds, we are apt to feel overwhelmed by the daunting task ahead of us. But remember what Paul said: "I can do all things through Christ which strengtheneth me" (Philippians 4:13).

Christ confirmed that when He taught in Jerusalem:

> Abide in me, and I in you. As the branch cannot bear fruit of itself, except it abide in the vine; no more can ye, except ye abide in me.
>
> I am the vine, ye *are* the branches: He that abideth in me, and I in him, the same bringeth forth much fruit: **for without me ye can do nothing.** (John 15:4–5)

But as Paul said, with Him we can do all things. Put Him to the test, or, as he challenged ancient Israel, "Prove me now herewith, saith the LORD of hosts" (Malachi 3:10).

The Lord is inviting us to challenge His proclamations. He has given over 250 promises in the Doctrine and Covenants alone of what He will do for his struggling, far-from-perfect Saints if they will only struggle on. Remember this famous verse: "I, the Lord, am bound when ye do what I say; but when ye do not what I say, ye have no promise" (D&C 82:10).

Further, remember this promise: "Be thou humble; and the Lord thy God shall lead thee by the hand, and give thee answer to thy prayers" (D&C 112:10).

The magnitude of the challenge we face is overwhelming—when we try to "go it alone." But putting life's challenges in perspective, we can make it with the Savior's help.

> For I am no respecter of persons, and will that all men shall know that the day speedily cometh; the hour is not yet, but is nigh at hand, when peace shall be taken from the earth, and the devil shall have power over his own dominion.
>
> And also the Lord shall have power over his saints, and **shall reign in their midst**, and shall come down in judgment upon Idumea, or the world. (D&C 1:35–36)

What a glorious opportunity to team up with the Lord as the curtain closes on the final act before the great Millennium begins. We know without doubt which side will win the battle against evil. The only question remaining is "which side we will be on?" Make the choice wisely. You may not get another chance.

About the Author

Brother Bott is married to the love of his life, Vickie (fifty years and counting). Together they have six children, sixteen grandchildren, and one great-granddaughter.

Brother Bott has bachelor's and master's degrees from Utah State University (a bachelor's in psychology, and a master's in secondary education) and a doctor's degree in educational leadership from BYU.

Brother Bott has served as a bishop, in two stake presidencies, and as a mission president. He served his first mission in Samoa. Since his retirement from BYU in 2012, he and his wife have served missions at BYU–Hawaii and in Sydney, Australia. They are currently preparing for another mission.

Brother Bott taught twenty years with CES in Utah and North Carolina. He taught nineteen years at BYU–Provo. He has authored many books and articles. His passion is teaching and counseling. He loves people and loves problem solving and creating new programs to help people succeed.

Notes

Notes

Notes